Anything for a Dull Moment

Poetry & Art

Michael Klam

GARDEN OAK PRESS
Rainbow, California

Garden Oak Press
1953 Huffstatler St., Suite A
Rainbow, CA 92028
760 728-2088
gardenoakpress.com *gardenoakpress@gmail.com*

First published by Garden Oak Press on November 15, 2020

ISBN-13: 978-1-7350556-2-6

Library of Congress Control Number: 2020942758

Printed in the United States of America

to **Jennifer Klam**

for all the late nights editing and posting and reposting

to **Anya, Henry,** and **Emma**

for all the times you've embraced our life of poetry and art

and to all the poets, musicians, performers, artists, volunteers, and MFA interns who have supported and graced the ***Poetry & Art Series*** through the years.

Anything
for a
Dull Moment

Poetry & Art

Michael Klam

edited by

Jennifer Chung Klam

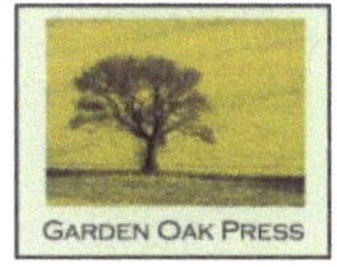

CONTENTS

Poetry & Art
selected poems, doodles, drawings, and paintings

Selected P&A Posters with Haiku

More Selected Poster/Flier Art

Poetry & Art

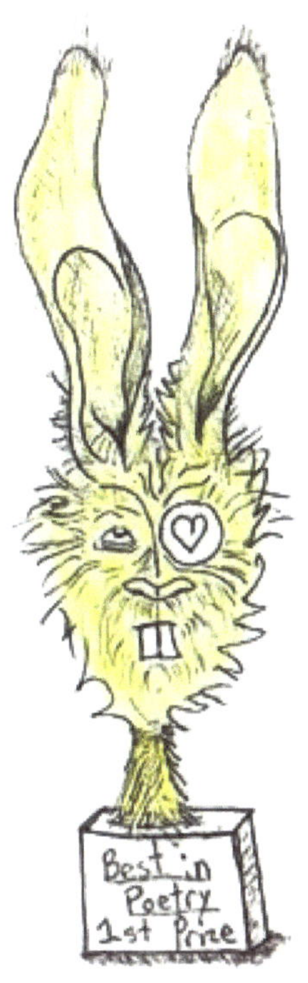

selected poems,
doodles, drawings, paintings

Folktales and Bits of Plastic

Watching crows all over the neighborhood
but not feeling an omen of change
or any sense of doom hailing from the sky.

Worried more about the people showing up
on the doorstep, creeping in through my devices,
racketeers, religious pimps, false doctors
agents of the arm-and-a-leg trash they
want me to know I "cannot live without."

Crows do not sell anything.
They just take, mostly eggs and bits of plastic.

I watch the crows and figure the house finches
and doves are cursed, but I do not
fear for the end.

On the contrary, when the marketers
and flimflam clerks come knocking,
I sense a swirling murder of capitalists.
I feast a focused eye on those who design and sell
the products and the packaging that will define
tomorrow's archaeology.

These predators don't want my flesh.
They want my mind.

I watch the crows whip around the neighborhood.

There are no monsters in the sky here.

Drinking from the Well

cheap vodka veteran
next to me
has been quiet
for a while

she feels the need to share:

"My mom told me that when I was a baby
in the womb I kicked her so hard
I broke her ribs."

I drink.

She talks over
a Bon Jovi song
I haven't heard since
the last time I was here:

"My mother used to tell me that story
in middle school to remind me of
how awful I was,
but I didn't believe her
until now."

she doesn't say another word,
and I don't respond.

I don't ask.

we drink
a lot
until I get up
and leave.

There Is No Chair in the Garage

This is no place to sit.

Here, we work.

The clubs come together.
The boards snap.
The beers drop quickly.

It will rain up there and soak the roof.
The wind will tear at the tiles.

There is no chair in the garage.
We stand.
We work.

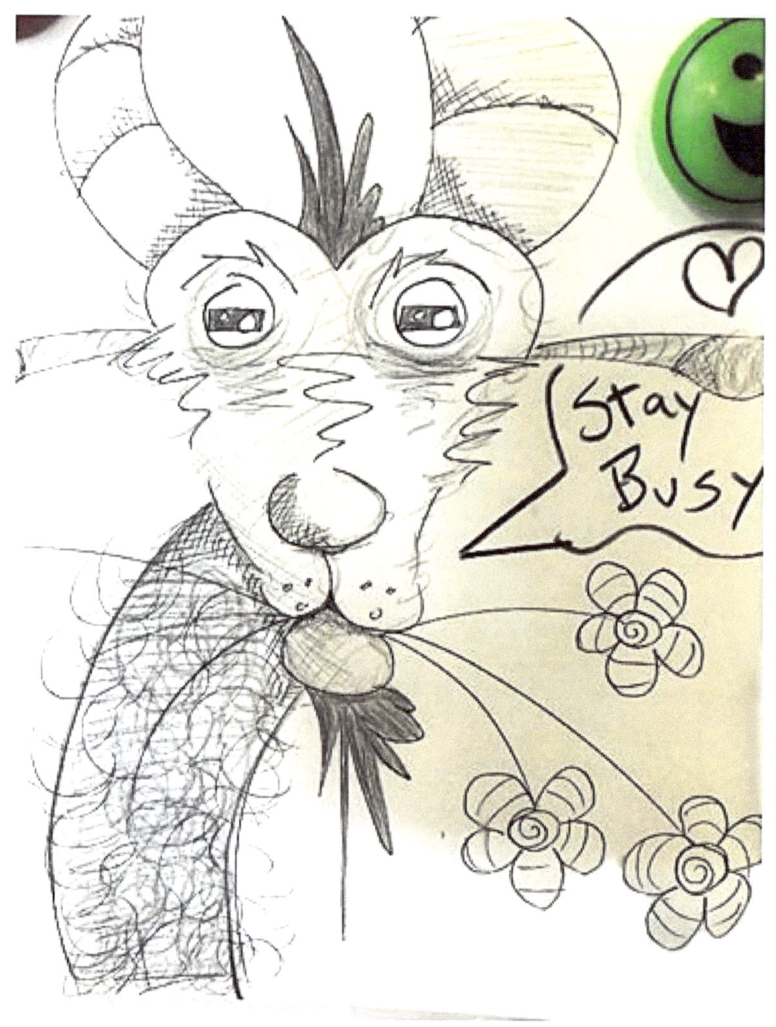

Goat Advice

Keep Your Head Down, Boy

Dad wants me to keep
my head down when I swing
a club.

Eyes wide open.
Ear to the ground.
Keep your head about you.

I swing and look up
before the club strikes.

I flub the shot.
It skitters along the ground
off-target.

He doesn't say
I told you so.

But his eyes mean it
and that smile
hits the mark.

The Moment She Really Left

when Emma drove away
for the first time
in a car she bought
in stealth
with my ex-wife
I felt so much terror
that I wanted to murder her
to avoid the pain
of watching her
leave every day
but she's okay
hopefully
no terrible accidents so far
except the screeching brakes
in my heart
and the crashes
that smash and burn
in my mind

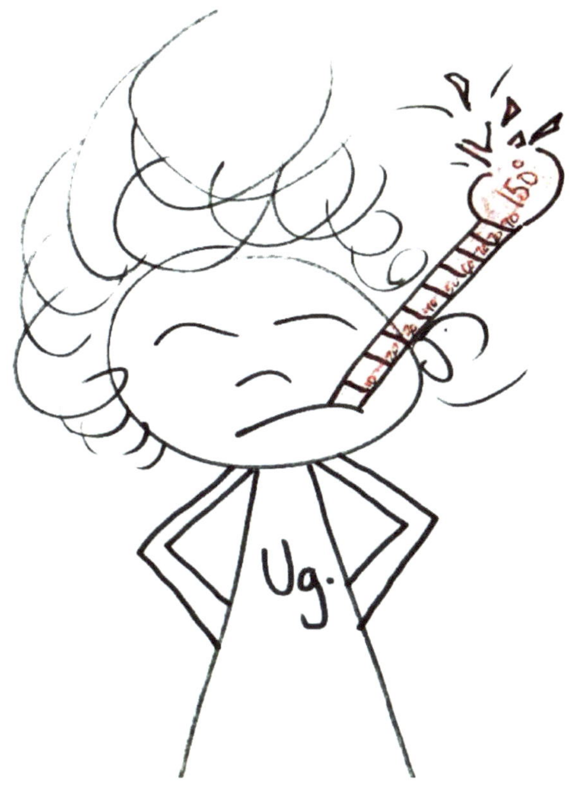

Ug.

Like Father Like Henry

when Henry was born
his mother almost
bled to death
but he turned out beautiful
and perfect
and prone to
questionable choices
like his father

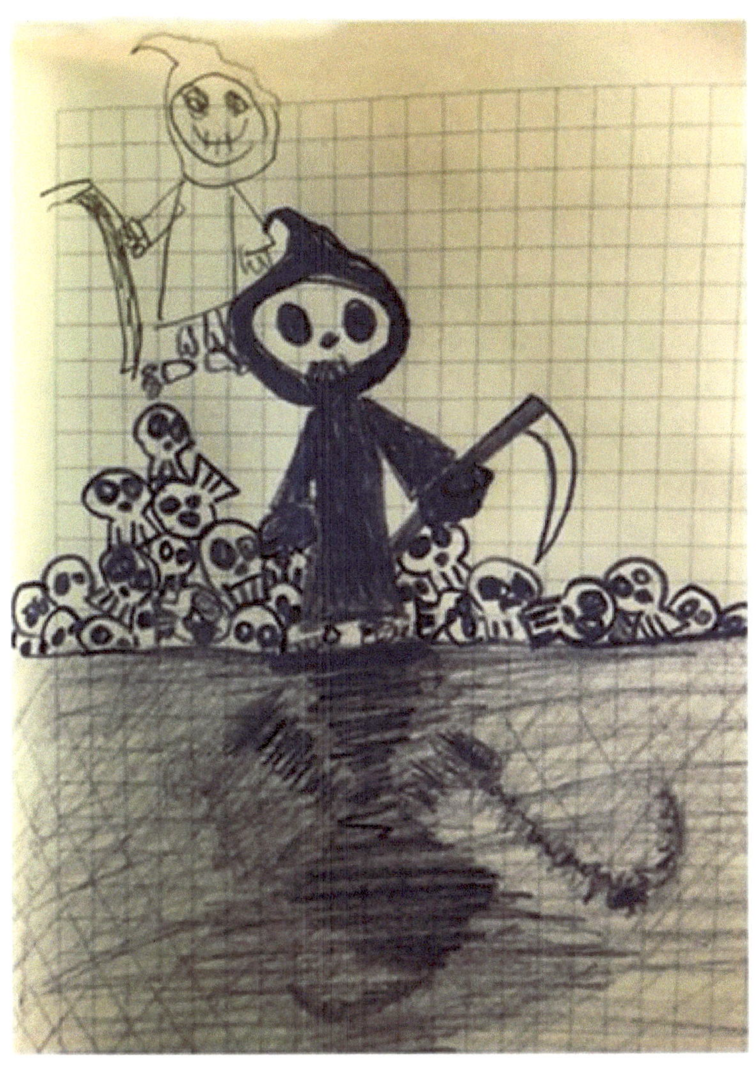

Be Nice, Son. Say Hello

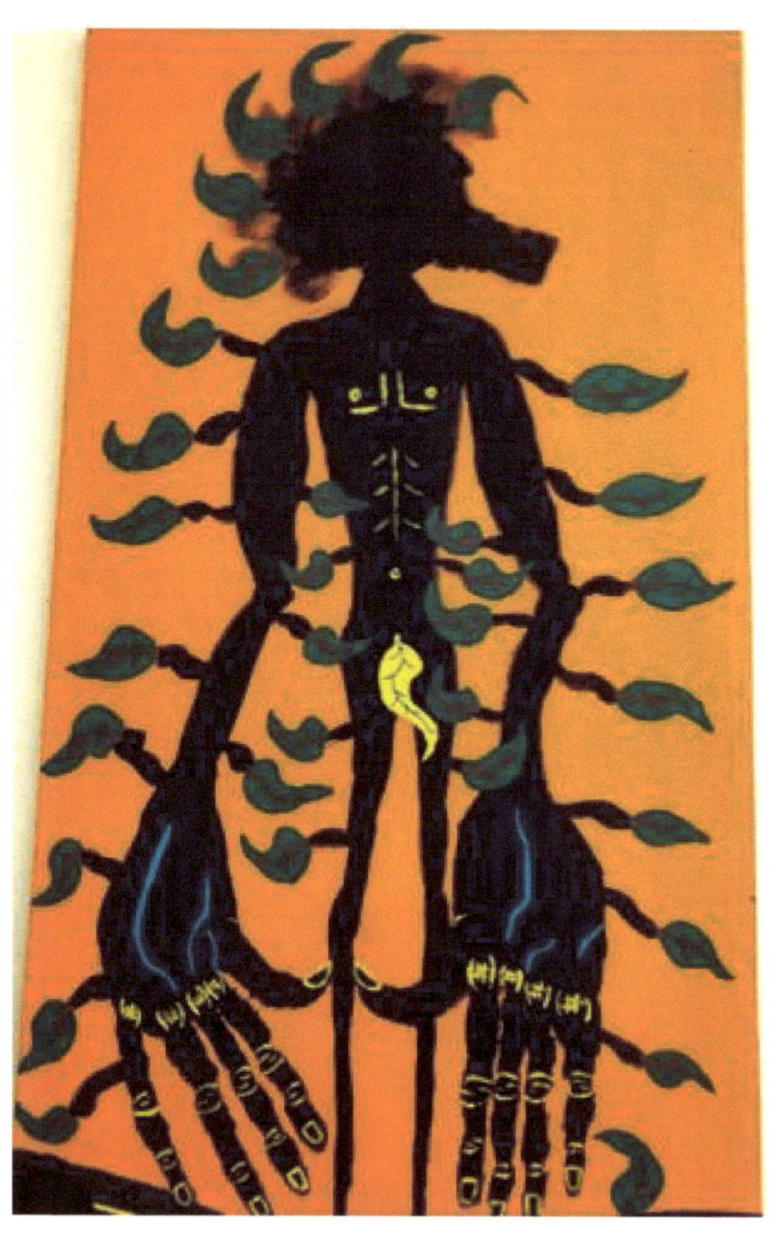

Don't Scratch

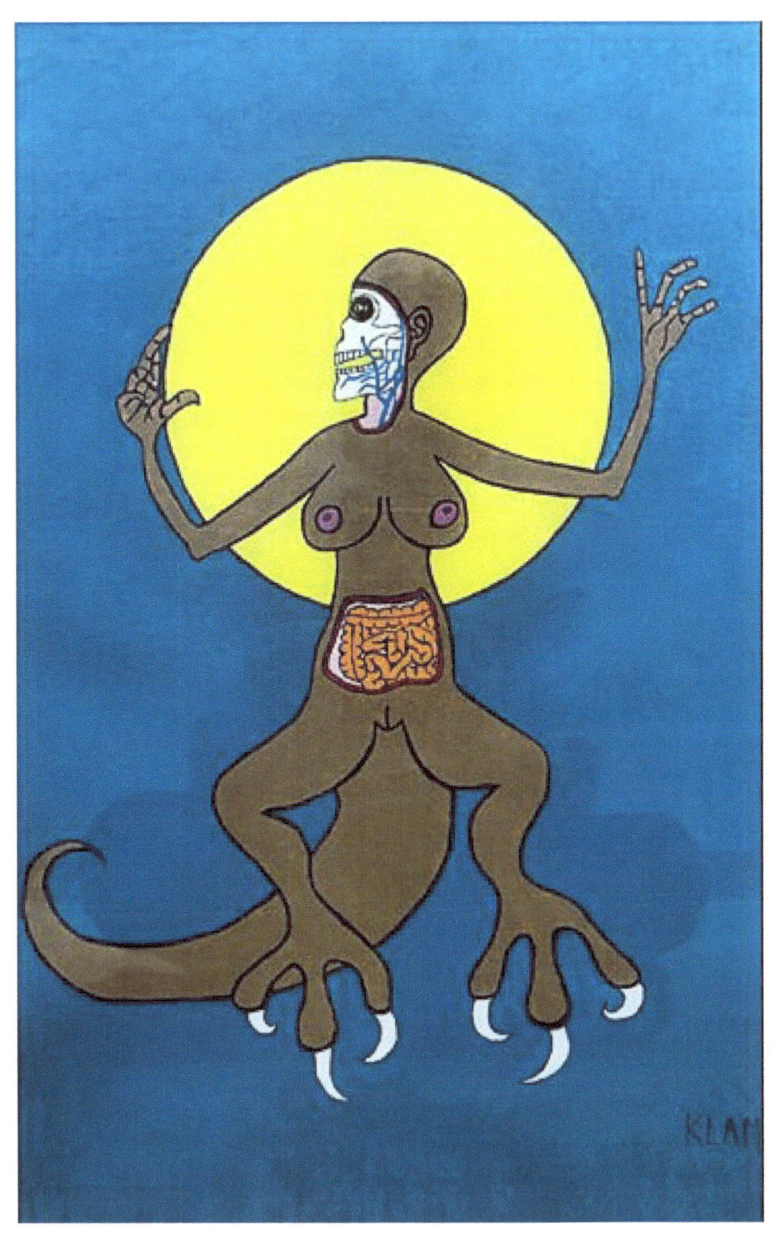

Retrato

Shooting the Pier

I fractured my hip
There's not much else to say
Love of my life
Pain of my life
It's all the same

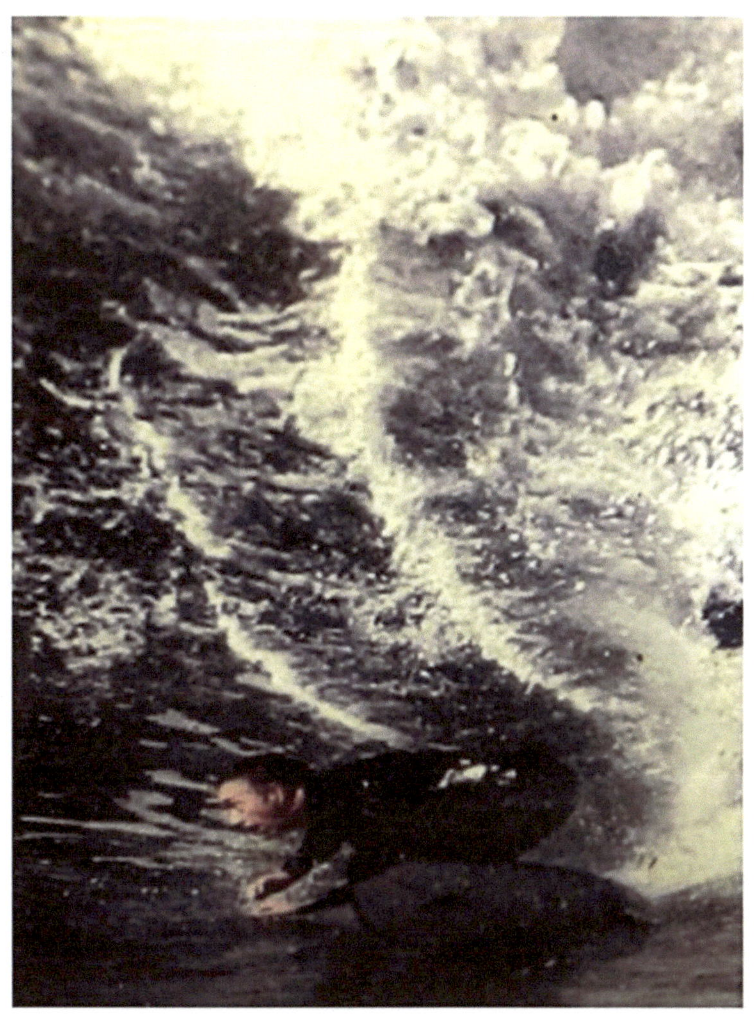

Bottom Turn with Skull in the Foam

Rest for the Wicked

today, Jennifer
I would like to usher in
the apocalypse
but I'm just not feeling up to it
and the sofa right now
glides thru heaven and earth
like a bed of feather down
plucked from the thighs
of chubby angels
exclusively for me

I should mow the lawn
empty the trash
replace the toilet seats
do the dishes

for you
I should tear down
this horrible world
squash a few righteous haters
in their bloody hats
and filthy boots
resist!

however,
my dearest love,
a good long nap is calling
and my lazy heart
must rest

smile
my queen
and remember
these drifting eyes
will see nothing ugly
today
and in my
temporary absence...
you will be free

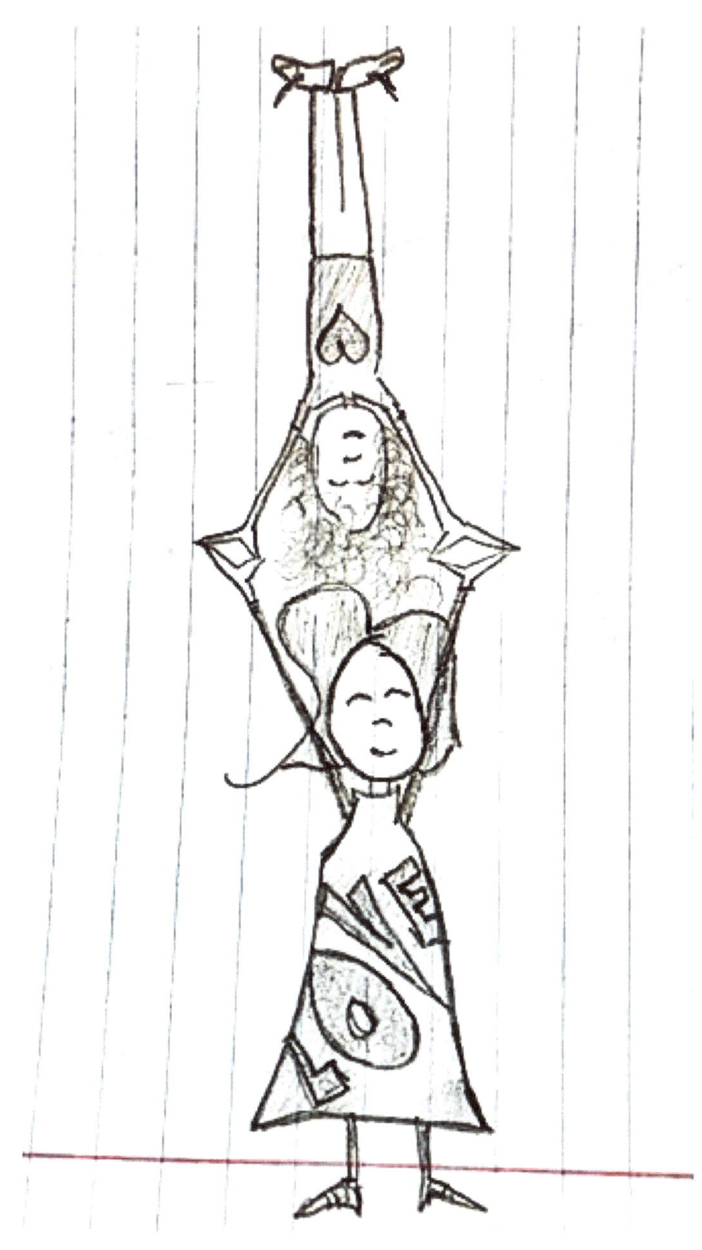

Anya and Mom

Nose Launch Intro

Drinking a perfectly poured Guinness
at the Strabane Golf Club
with Dad

Jock behind the bar
overjoyed because we brought
Milk Duds and Kool-Aid from the States

The lads come over
to say hello to Dad
and find out who I am

They are all blitzed, several pints in
and the room booms
with slurred voices and laughter

Tommy comes over
to pay Dad a pound he lost
in pairs competition

Jock and Dad, like best friends,
tell each other lovingly
to go fuck themselves

Carol swings in
with score card and smiles
and good cheer

Then Declan grows a few balls
rumbles up to us
and launches half a quart of snot

and a pint of drool out of his head
while trying to manufacture the word Hello
to introduce himself

Declan says a lot in the next two minutes
I don't understand him at all
but the boys laugh hard so I laugh too

I am all at once utterly out of place
and completely at home here
somewhere between the drink

and the frothing and belly laughter
I was born on this wet island
in the middle of this unrelenting sea

the weather of our people is our people
unpredictable, tempestuous, beautiful
more often cracking and pouring than calm

Lizzie shows up to take us home
we step outside, the wind howls, and all the way home
the laurels and the firs dance like drunken fools

Whiplash 9 to 5

the boss has wicked eyes from a lifetime of faking kindness

she hates herself more than the rest

wicked eyes and a whiplash smile to twist some necks

get the job done

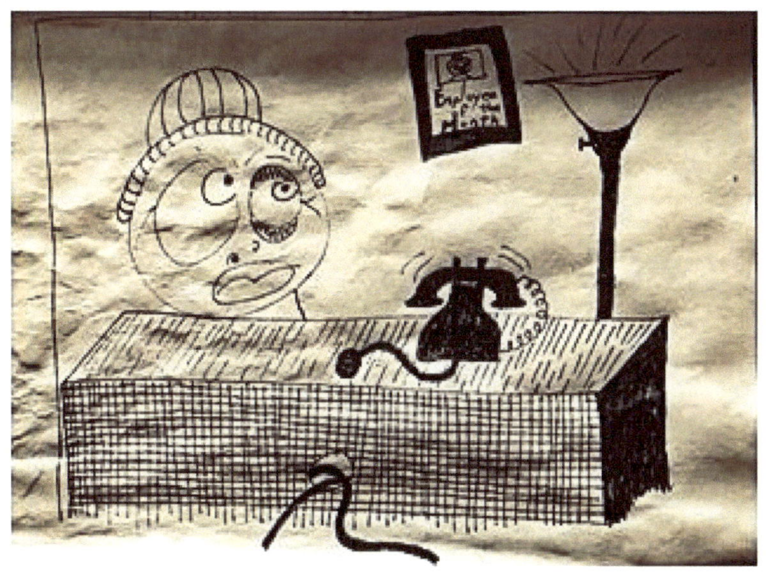

Employee of the Month

A Nice Stone

I bought a diamond ring once
with bloody knuckles
from punching the wrong part
of a wall.

In Hollywood
the protagonist
grieving or drunk
knocks a hole in the pain.

I hit a stud
and tore the skin off the bones.

The owner of the jewelry store
seemed unfazed
like he had seen it before.
He said very little.

I said nothing
bleeding on the pen
as I wrote the check.

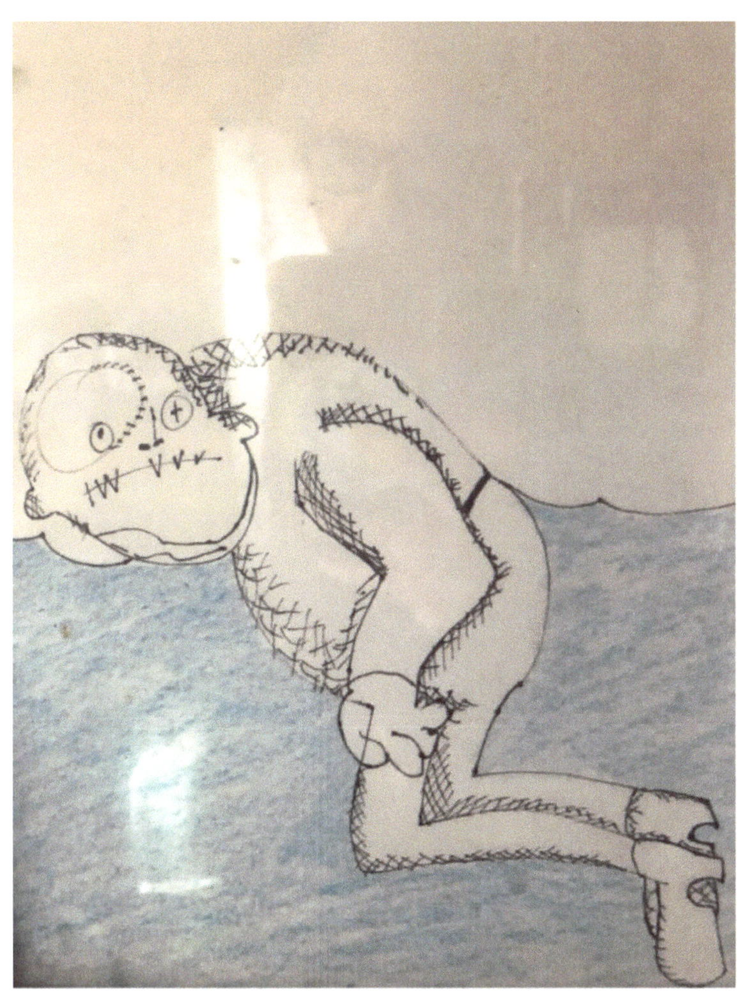

Drowning

Lazy by Natural Selection

I sit and watch
my life go by
and wish I could
shake myself
awake
do something
anything
but sit here
dreaming

Then,
of course,
when I get too busy,
I miss
my old self.

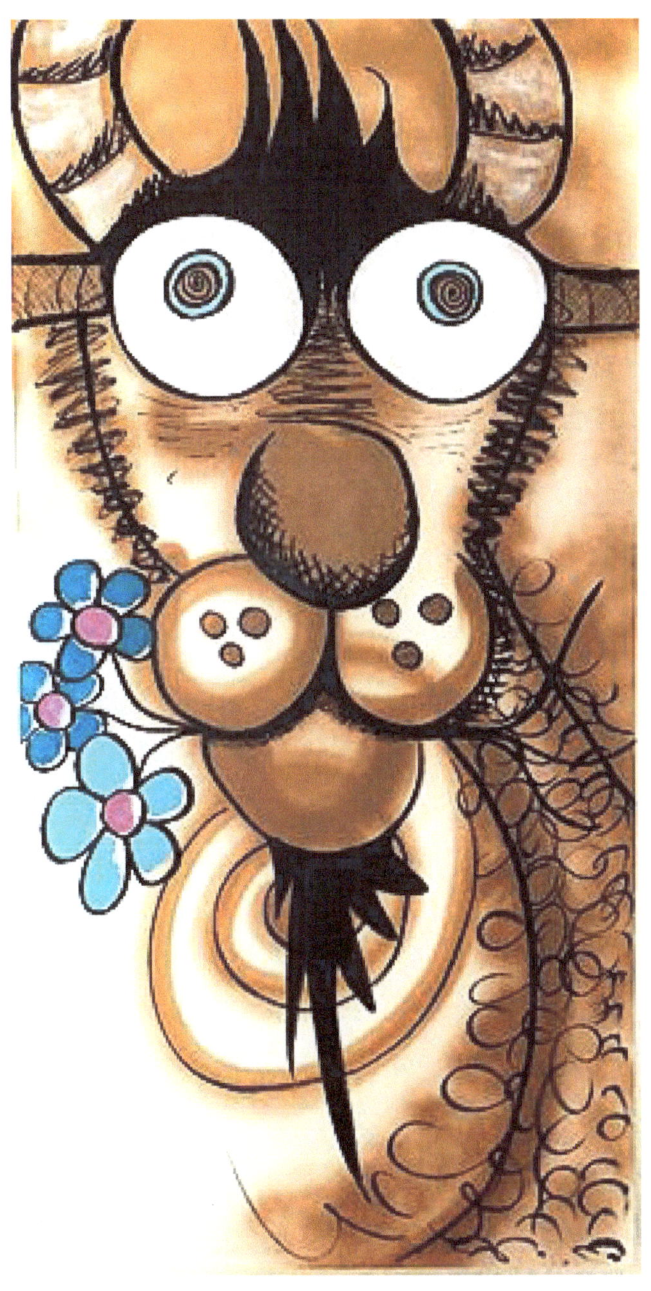

Greatest of All Time

Touring Ireland with Me Da

dad won't let me drive
says it's unsafe
yet he has a death wish
on the road

he tailgates like he's blind
hits the brakes like
death is throwing darts
at his head...

nowhere to go
but grip me arse
into the seat
and pray

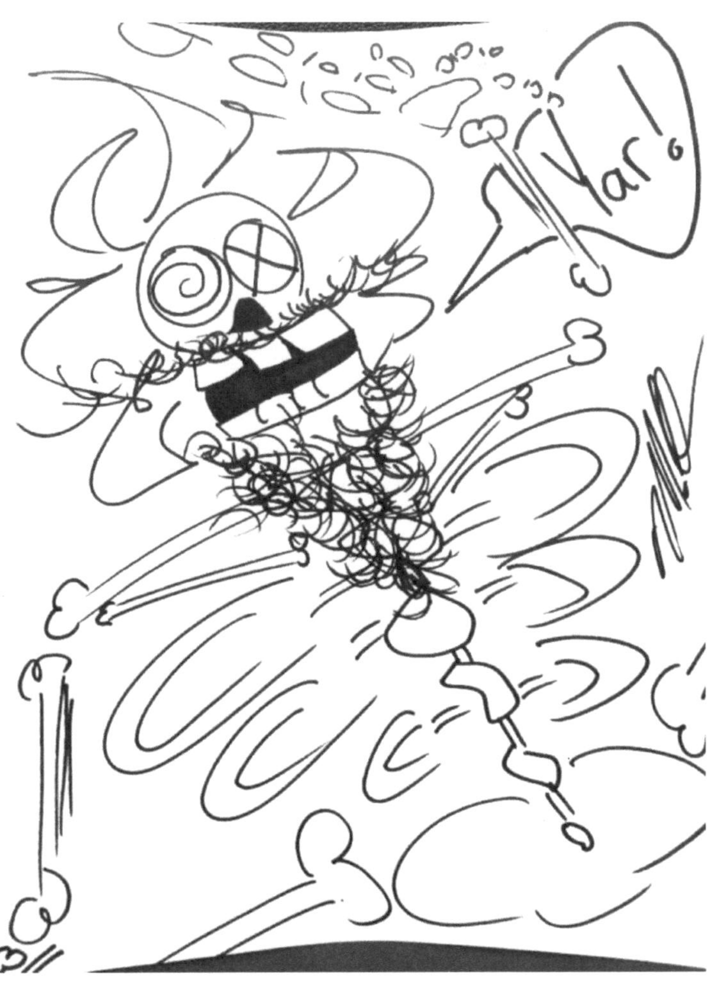

Yar!

Summer Vacation Abroad, 2019

There have been
four mass shootings
in the US
since we have been
here in Strabane.

Dayton, El Paso, Gilroy,
a Mississippi Walmart.

America.

What do we say
to our family and friends here?

We are sad?
We are ugly?

All those guns.
All those bibles.
All those backward,
decent, God-and-skin-color-
fearing-folk
who voted for
white nationalism
when they voted
for Trump
but will remind you
that they voted
to "Make America
Great Again"
and to "Build a Wall."

Our neighbors.
Our friends.
Our families.

They will never accept their
responsibility in this.

What is ours?

Guns and money.
Guilt and shame
buried
in political mud
molten rhetoric
shifting landmines
everywhere
in a war
everyone knows is raging
a war right here
buried in the dirt.

Fear is left.

What do we say?

We are afraid?

We vote, I guess.
We protest, I suppose.
We speak up, again.

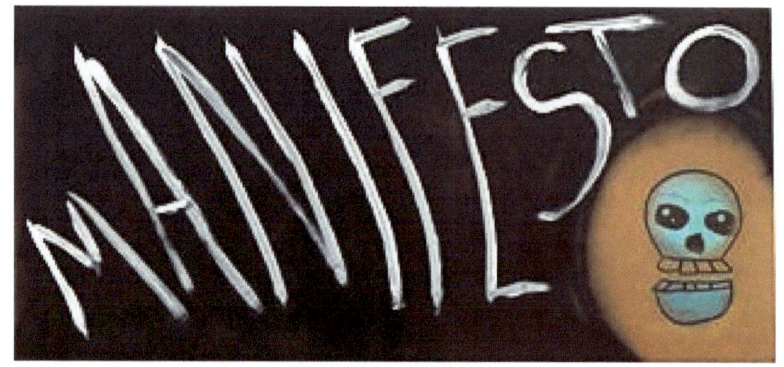

Manifesto

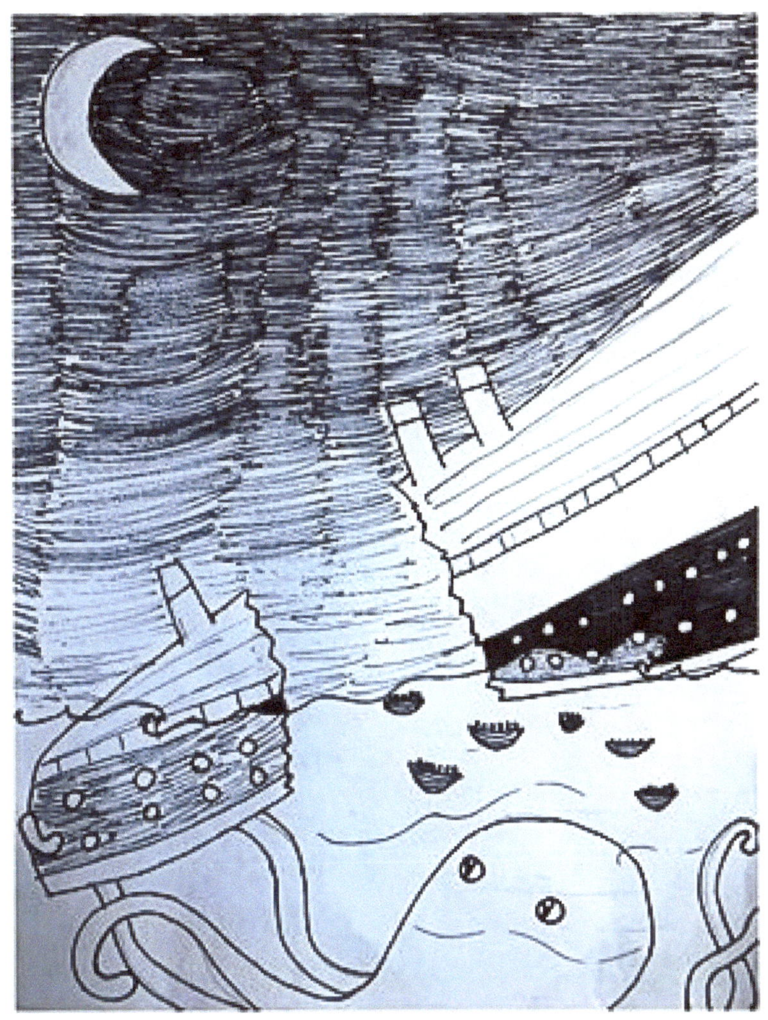

Titanic by Anya Klam

Titanic Gift Shop

Fifteen hundred souls
did not go straight to the bottom
when the Titanic sank.

The passengers wailed,
tore at each other's skin,
gulped down their sins
until salty ice filled their lungs
dragged them into the abyss.

Before the Titanic cracked in half
families held each other
one last time.

There were no politics in the *I Love You's*:
Lovers died with their best friends.
Children drowned without mercy.

Now, at the gift shop,
tourists can buy a wee Titanic
floating in an emerald shamrock
on a silver chain
for 99 pounds (about $125 US).

Travelers can read all about
the "Great Men" who sent ships
to founder, to dance
with mines and torpedoes
and icebergs.

The lovers of Jack and Rose
can meet the slave laborers
who banged molten rivets
for twelve hours a day,
on bread and tea alone, and discover
how the constant clanging
drove the workers deaf and mad, their poverty
bringing them back day after day
to ensure Titanic would
shove off into her fate.

There, today, in the Titanic Centre
a children's book explains
that two-and-a-half miles down
the Atlantic eats the Queen of the Seas:

Halomonas titanicae,
microbes, tiny bacteria,
grind the great coffin to dust
leaving only
mixed memories from the deep
and tawdry
pricey souvenirs
in the gift shop.

Boarding with Anya Klam

Anya glides by
on a stand-up paddle board

elegant as a pelican
ruling the water

I trail behind, sliding over the amber,
the sunrise diamonds, proud papa

as San Diego Bay awakens
I follow Anya into the morning sun

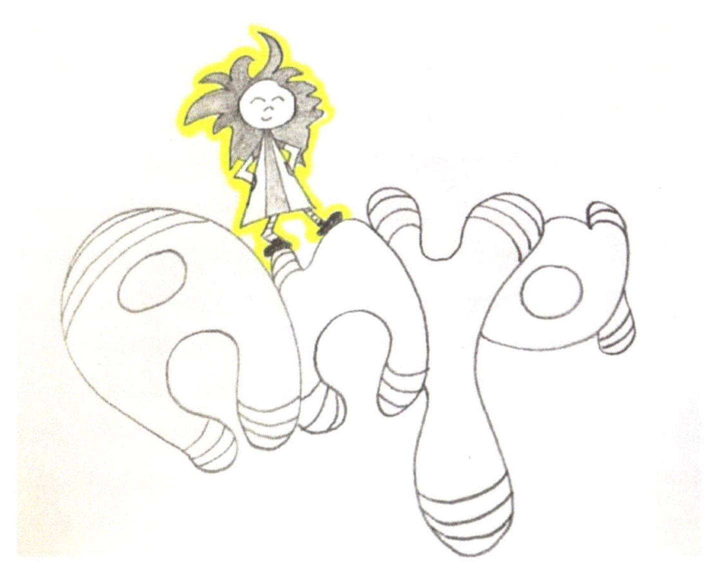

Anya Gold Level

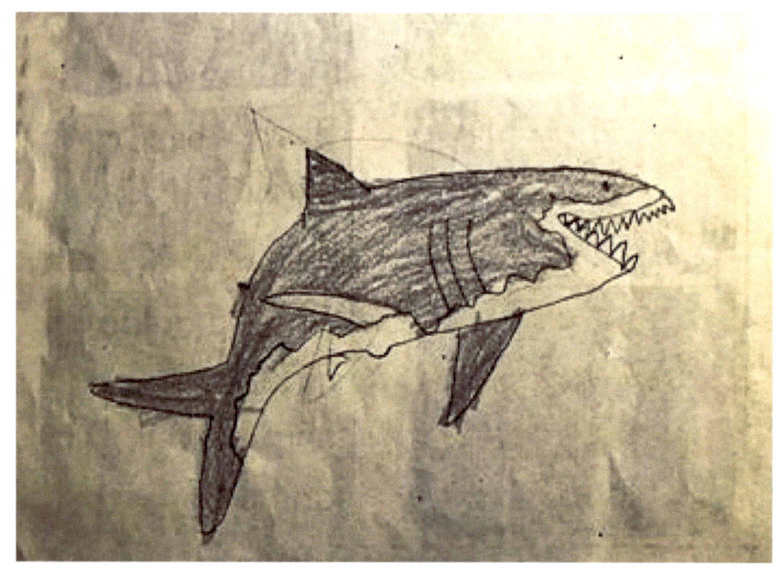

Anya's Shark

Love Letter to the Poetry Editor

There has to be
a book binding formula
a ratio of times a reader
flips through
and ends up
on the same page
a scientific formula
that guarantees
my poem and my ego
will be satisfied
every time the reader
opens her book
mathematically:
flip velocity plus glue density divided by
spinal tension with a quantum
luck variable factored in...
Dear editor,
Please do the math.
Find the grip
in your anthology's core
and put my poem there.

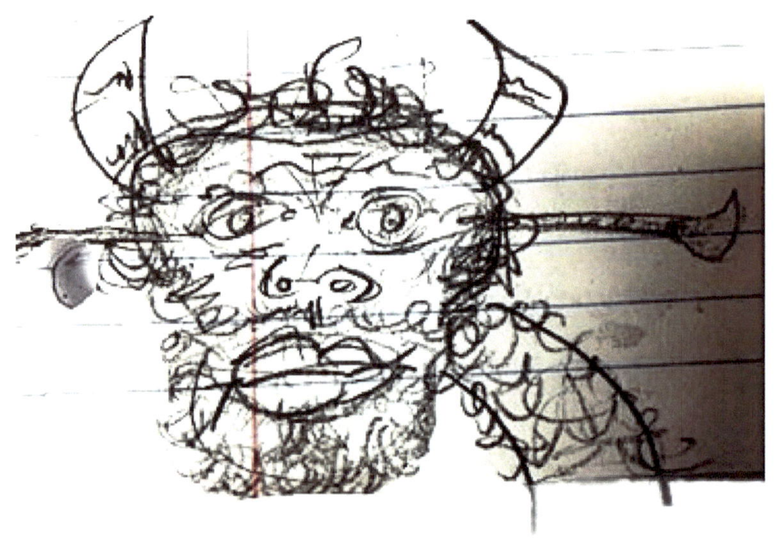

Self Portrait in the Margin

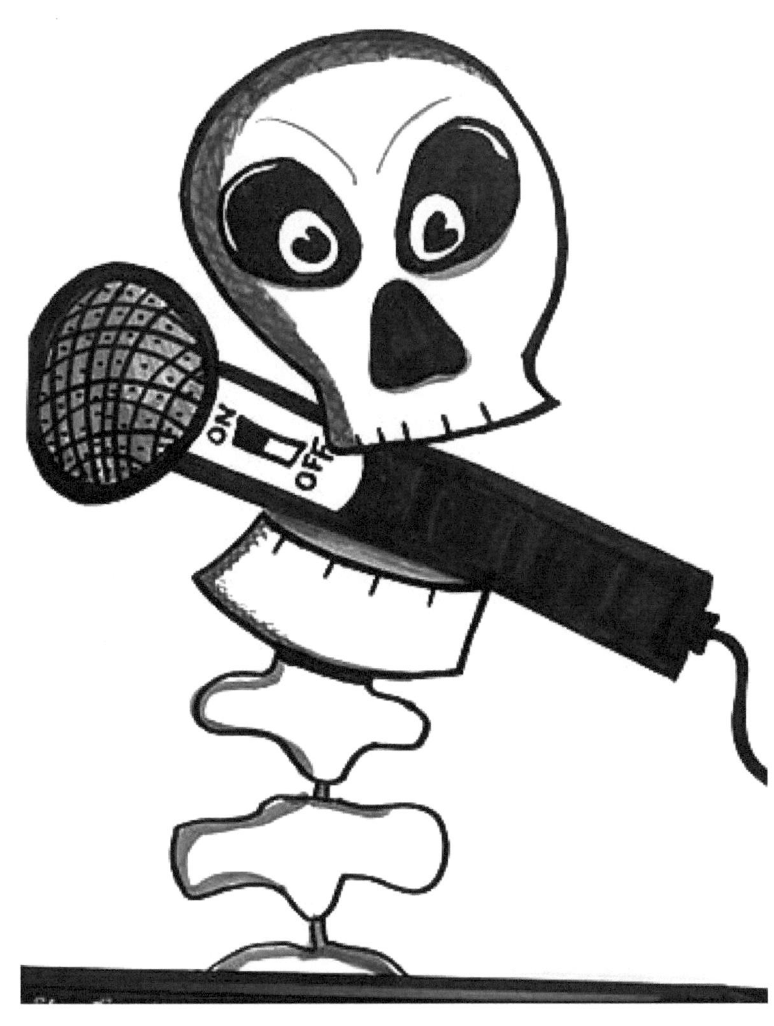

Sometimes You Eat the Mic. Sometimes the Mic Eats You.

Karaoke Suicidal

James
who is a singer
but never sings
leans over to me
half-tanked
half-an-hour into karaoke
at the Ould Sod
somewhere between
the divine voices
and the horrid squelching
and says,
"Michael, It's a fine line
between life and the pistol"
and I agree:
a line like a distant fiber
for some
a line like the Grand Canyon
for others
a wide fine line
to be walked
balanced upon
by the balding rock star
the karaoke king
who charges the mic
like a fish chasing live bait
to sing a Dean Martin version
of *Funky Cold Medina*
and it's sink and swim
half music
half gurgling distortion
brave
brave liquid soul
sucking through the lips
belting out through the gills
having moments of absolute brilliance
as the brimming bodies of the bar
fill with music

and the room floods
with spirit
and the karaoke culture
applauds its own genius
alive
like the line itself
the fine line
between life
and the pistol

Clear Cut

Rough mountain
reduced to gravel roadway
cold ash

When the trees
fell in the forest
did the machines
drown out the sound?

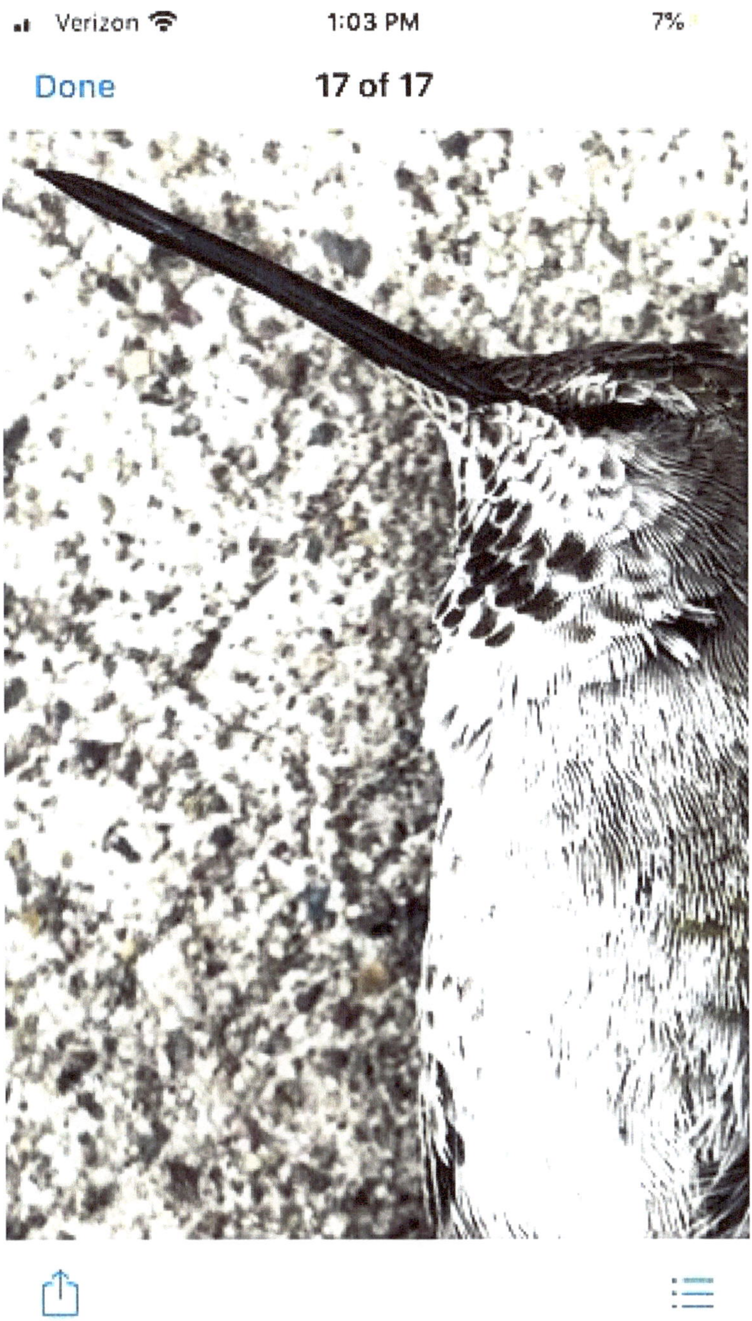

Verizon 1:03 PM 7%

Hummingword

Urban Rainbows

I saw a slow mist
make the street black
and glossy.

Many colors streaked
from wet curbs,
and I felt sick.

My little girl pointed,
"Look, Poppa!
Rainbows!"

A city bus
cut through
the chemical slick.

Death by Palm Tree in Costa Rica, Almost

as the sun baked
the pelicans hunted
the needle fish fled

a coconut fell
splashed cobbles
in all directions

the jungle went quiet
for a moment
like taking a breath

without warning
a sudden orchestration
of popping and cracking

a six-story palm tree toppled
out of the jungle
exploded onto the beach
into the tide
right in front of me
like a whip
coming down from the sky
to part the waters

the sweet gulf rushed up and around
as if claiming a piece
of the rainforest
victorious

I sat down on the cobblestones
and watched waves dance
in the fronds

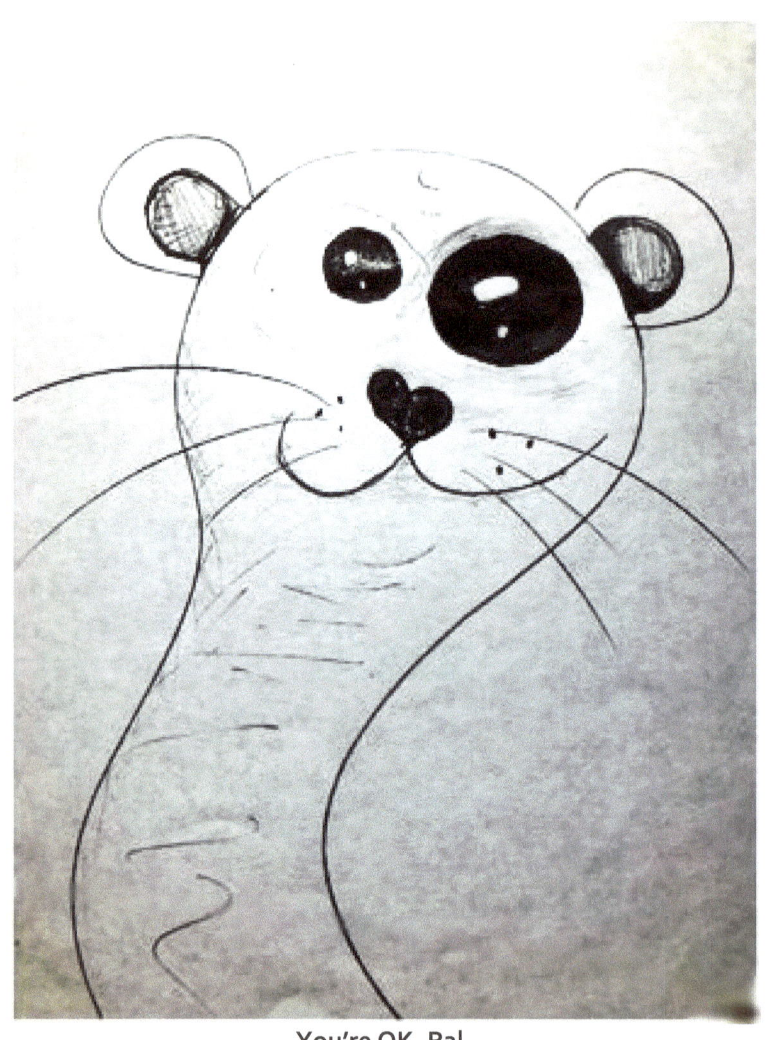

You're OK, Pal

listening around the table

those
talking the most
have the most
to hide
according to the quiet ones
who know that if the talkers
shut their mouths
the room will go silent
and the silence
will give everyone away
all of us
we are
only as sick as
our secrets
and
ultimately
there is
no escape
but maybe
for a moment
of relief
            a good story
we should
go ahead
and keep telling
good stories

Irish Summer, St George's Market

the musician kills
to no applause

every language fills the market
laughter too, good cheer

salmon and haddock
stink up one side

old maps of Ireland
gone stale on the other

I haven't heard Otis' song in years
Sittin' on the dock of the bay

wasting time in Saint George's
with no plan to buy anything

people-watching
my favorite game

somewhere between the vendors
and the tourists there is peace

humanity retreats
politics take a break

food from every continent
dances through the air with the music

I left my home in Georgia
and I headed for the 'Frisco Bay

I lose the girls, they've sailed off
I turn 360 degrees / one slow panorama

I can't see them
but I don't feel lost here

drifting along / soon enough
my family appears

watching the ships roll in
watching the tide roll away

we take pictures of the fish
laugh at their weird, ugly mouths

we slip out of the market
to stroll along River Lagan

here in the land of downpours
and soft days

the water is dark like Guinness
and bullets do not rain down on us today

hungover on a train to Belfast

pasty man
has been telling stories
for an hour

his voice beats on me

I'll never remember
what he says

but I'll always remember
seeing his purple blood
through his magic skin

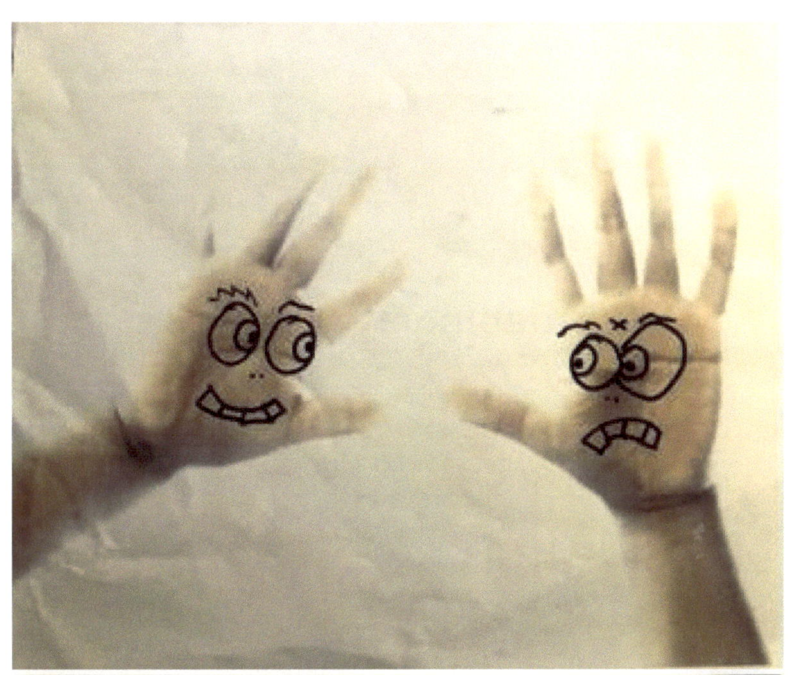

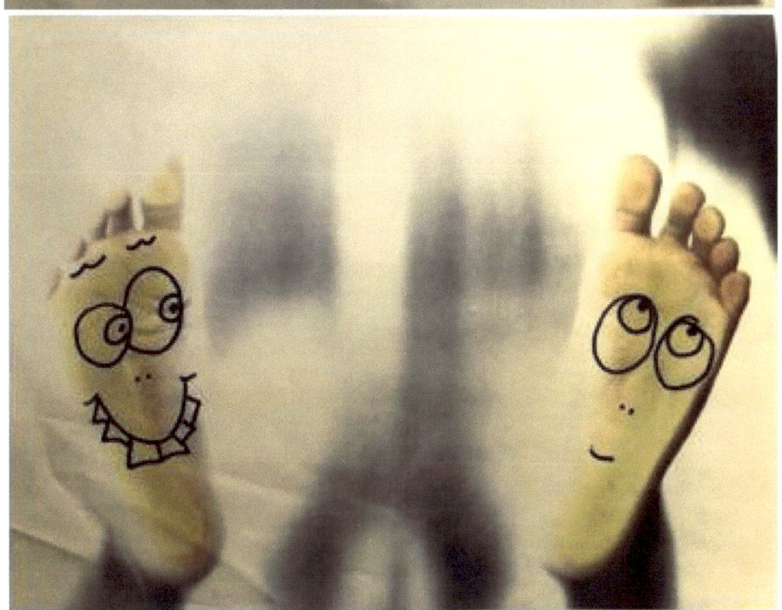

Relationships, Hand and Foot

Gardening as an Atheist

I swear to your gods
when I grab at ugly weeds
they look up and dodge

Selected P&A Posters
with Haiku

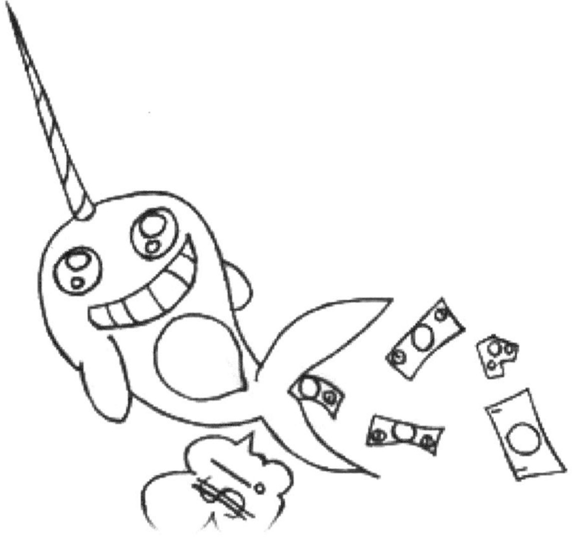

The following pages contain haiku (loosely defined) poems about select Poetry & Art Series (P&A) events over the years. I have organized and hosted P&A since 2001, and the series features poets, artists, performers, and musicians.

I wrote the haiku and drew many of the images. Jennifer Klam and I designed the fliers – Jennifer working her Photoshop magic – and Anya Klam contributed some of the best (and cutest) drawings. Some of the fliers include reconstructed art found online.

Each haiku precedes its corresponding flier(s).

To find out more about the P&A series, see pictures, and read poems by the featured authors, visit *poetryandartsd.com* and search for Broken Anchor Poetry.

Broken Anchor Poetry

Poetry & Art Series

these poems, these shows
never told the whole story
just moments in time

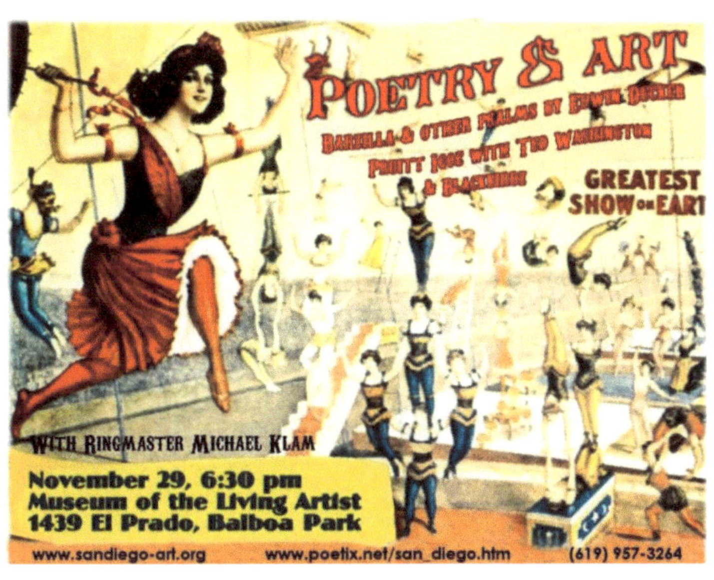
POETRY & ART
GREATEST
SHOW ON EART
WITH RINGMASTER MICHAEL KLAM
November 29, 6:30 pm
Museum of the Living Artist
1439 El Prado, Balboa Park
www.sandiego-art.org
www.poetix.net/san_diego.htm
(619) 957-3264

Fire

poet grrrls step up
vocal fuego heart and soul
take no prisoners

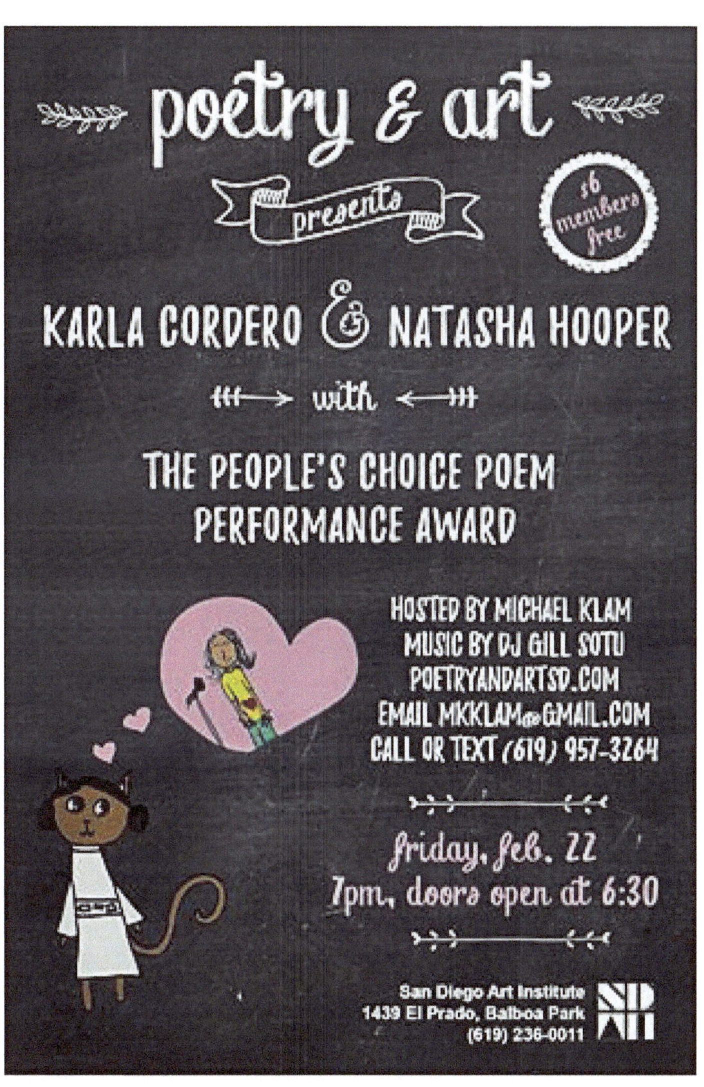
poetry & art
presents
$6 members free
KARLA CORDERO & NATASHA HOOPER
with
THE PEOPLE'S CHOICE POEM PERFORMANCE AWARD
HOSTED BY MICHAEL KLAM
MUSIC BY DJ GILL SOTU
POETRYANDARTSD.COM
EMAIL MKKLAM@GMAIL.COM
CALL OR TEXT (619) 957-3264
Friday, Feb. 22
7pm, doors open at 6:30
San Diego Art Institute
1439 El Prado, Balboa Park
(619) 236-0011

Full Body Slam

why wouldn't poetry
and wrestling go together?
perfect sense to me

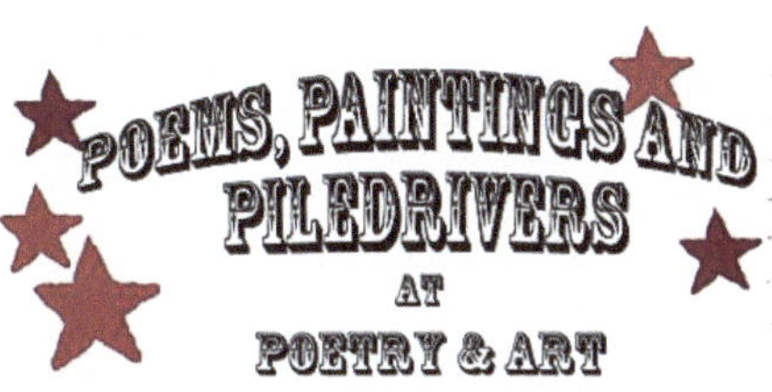

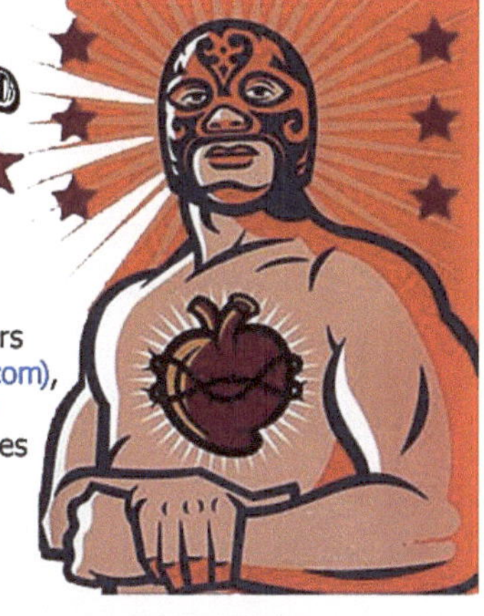

Live painting smackdown!

A schizophrenic battle of words and colors with Rudos y Técnicos (www.aztecgoldtv.com), Victor Payan and Sandra Pocha Peña! Watch them battle it out with paintbrushes on a blank canvas!

Hosted by San Diego author Michael Klam
Nachos! Salsa! Guacamole! Open mic!
Connect 3 with Ginger Placek
Music by Zuri Waters
$5, members free; (619) 957-3264

GET READY TO RUMBLE!

Wednesday, Aug. 16 at 6:30 p.m.
Museum of the Living Artist
Balboa Park

No Heroes

anarchy offends
poetasters, hypocrites
smells like teen spirit

Poetry & Art presents
The Book of Books by Jimmy Jazz
Saturday, Nov. 5, 7pm
Doors open at 6:30pm
featuring readings from
Steve Abee (LA), Kimberly Dark (SD), Rich Ferguson (LA), Minerva (LA), Shawna Kenney (LA), Gill Sotu (SD), and Ted Washington (SD)
Plus the People's Choice Poem Performance Awards
$50 cash prizes, winners chosen by the audience in a secret ballot
$5 or free with snacks or libations to share
San Diego Art Institute
1439 El Prado, Balboa Park
Hosted by Michael Klam
for more info or to sign up
call or text 619-457-3264

Handing Out Tens Like Candy

slam poets, fearless,
I do not know why, maybe
they just feel at home

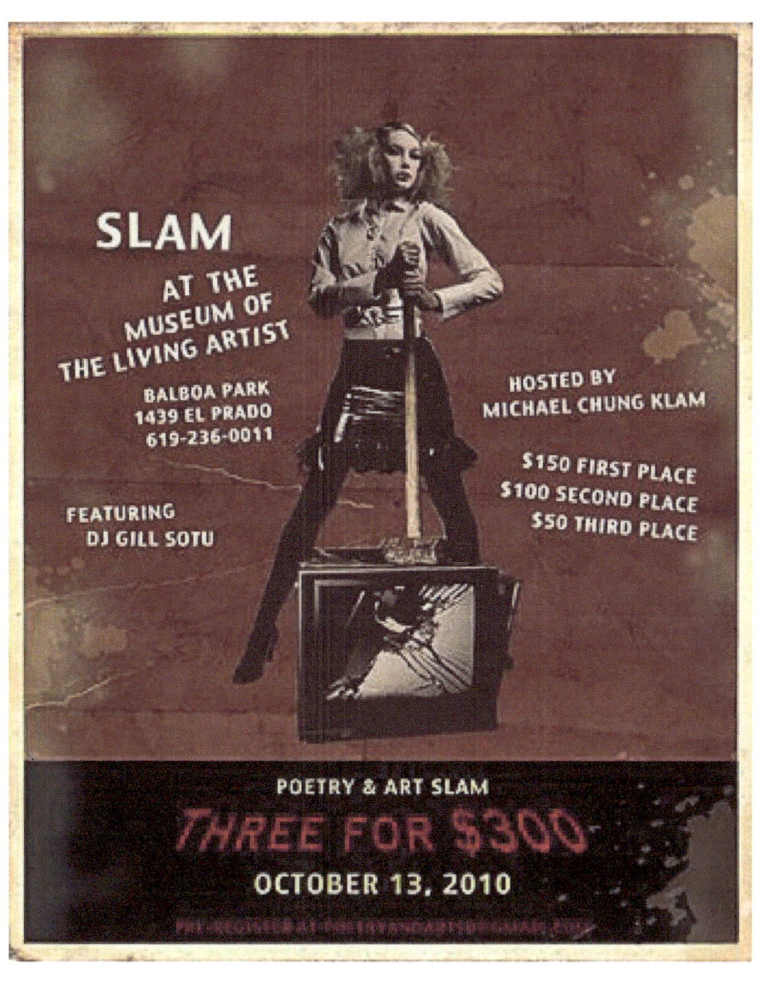
SLAM
AT THE
MUSEUM OF
THE LIVING ARTIST
BALBOA PARK
1439 EL PRADO
619-236-0011
FEATURING
DJ GILL SOTU
HOSTED BY
MICHAEL CHUNG KLAM
$150 FIRST PLACE
$100 SECOND PLACE
$50 THIRD PLACE
POETRY & ART SLAM
THREE FOR $300
OCTOBER 13, 2010

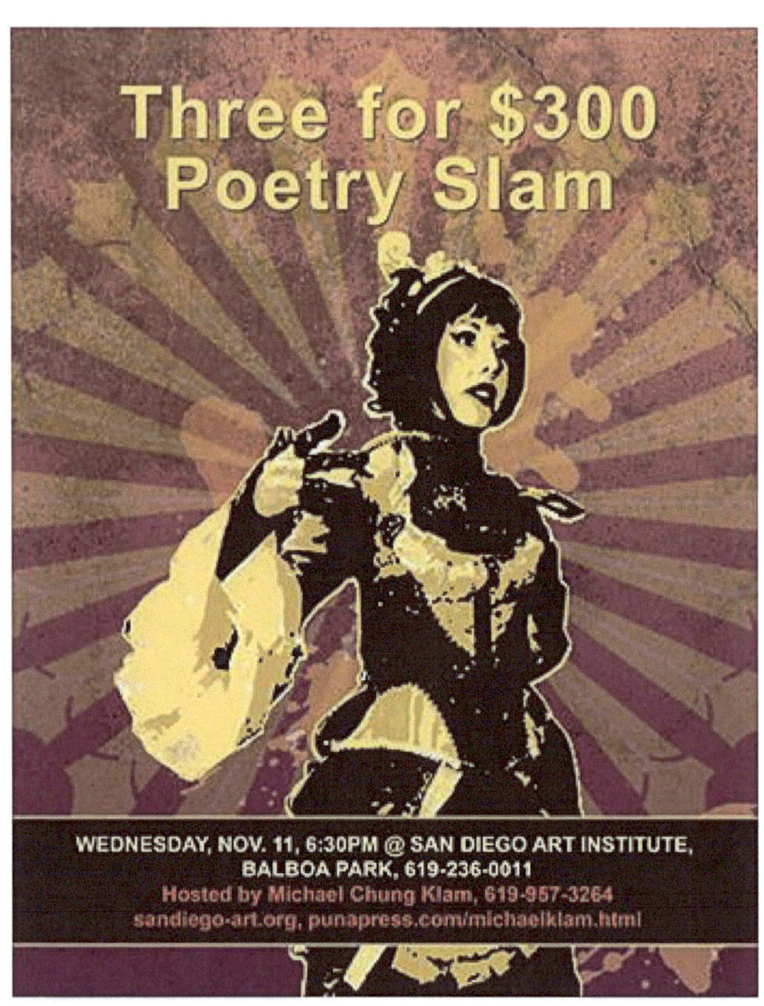
Three for $300
Poetry Slam
WEDNESDAY, NOV. 11, 6:30PM @ SAN DIEGO ART INSTITUTE,
BALBOA PARK, 619-236-0011
Hosted by Michael Chung Klam, 619-957-3264
sandiego-art.org, punapress.com/michaelklam.html

Poetry & Art

presents THE $1,000 YOUTH & ADULT POETRY PERFORMANCE PRIZE

plus THREE $50 PEOPLE'S CHOICE PRIZES CHOSEN BY THE AUDIENCE BY SECRET BALLOT

HOSTED BY MICHAEL KLAM, MUSIC BY DJ GILL SOTU
FOR MORE INFO VISIT POETRYANDARTSD.COM
EMAIL MKKLAM@GMAIL.COM
CALL OR TEXT (619) 957-3264

Friday, Oct. 26
7pm, Doors open 6:30pm

$6, MEMBERS FREE

San Diego Art Institute
1439 El Prado, Balboa Park
(619) 236-0011

SD AI

Ilya Kaminsky's Voice

Ilya comes smiling
takes over the mic as if
sound traveled lightly

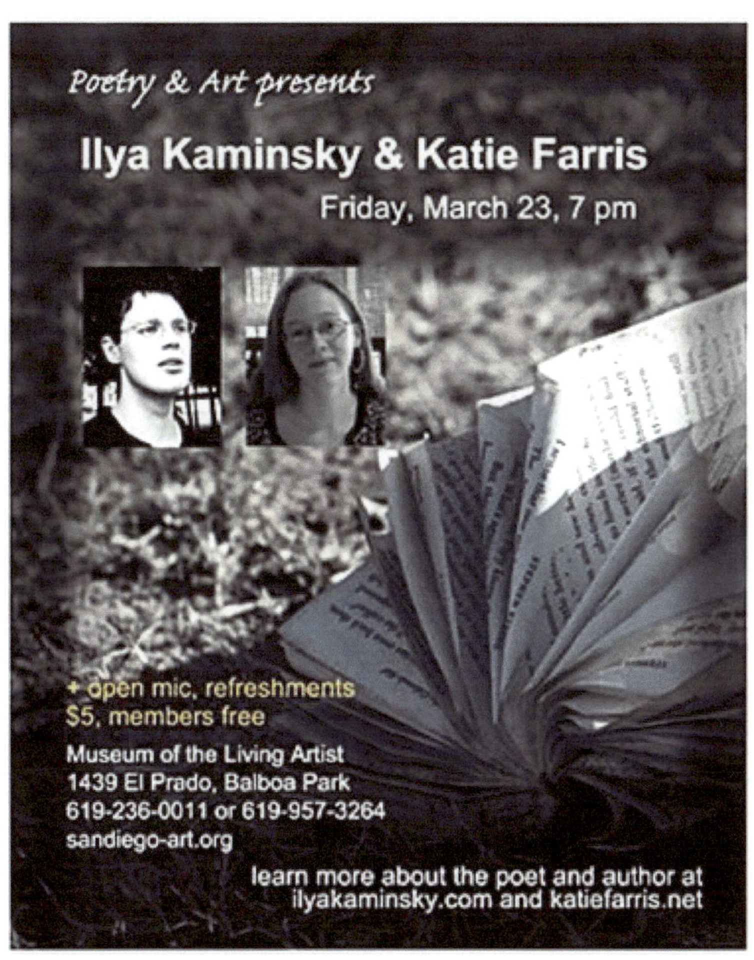

Poetry & Art presents
Ilya Kaminsky & Katie Farris
Friday, March 23, 7 pm
+ open mic, refreshments
$5, members free
Museum of the Living Artist
1439 El Prado, Balboa Park
619-236-0011 or 619-957-3264
sandiego-art.org
learn more about the poet and author at
ilyakaminsky.com and katiefarris.net

Nope

pulp fiction flier
denied by featured poet
"take them down," she said

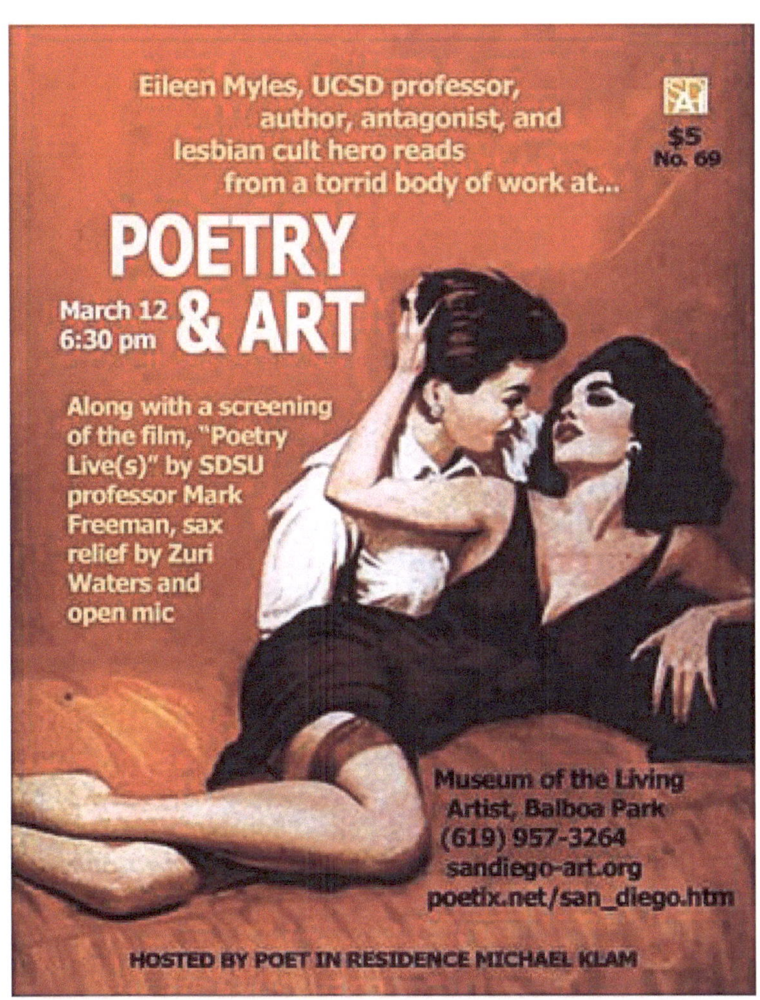
Eileen Myles, UCSD professor,
author, antagonist, and
lesbian cult hero reads
from a torrid body of work at...
$5
No. 69
POETRY
& ART
March 12
6:30 pm
Along with a screening
of the film, "Poetry
Live(s)" by SDSU
professor Mark
Freeman, sax
relief by Zuri
Waters and
open mic
Museum of the Living
Artist, Balboa Park
(619) 957-3264
sandiego-art.org
poetix.net/san_diego.htm
HOSTED BY POET IN RESIDENCE MICHAEL KLAM

No Illusions, Recycled Flier, Spared No Expense

Sordid Tales poet,
the junky literati
said Ewe won the night

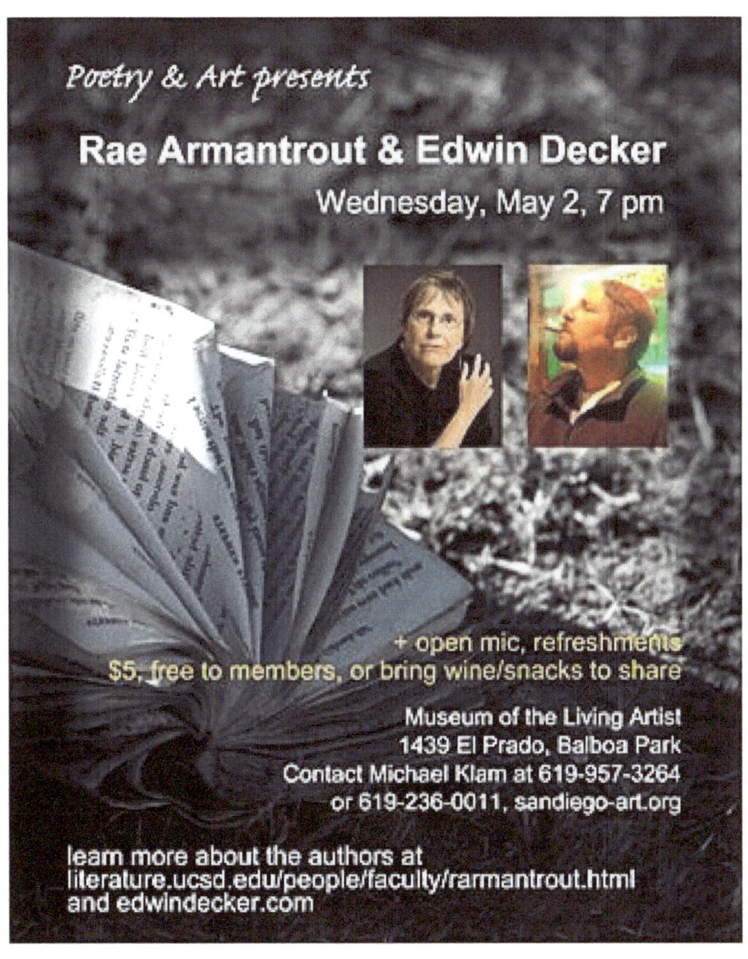
Poetry & Art presents
Rae Armantrout & Edwin Decker
Wednesday, May 2, 7 pm
+ open mic, refreshments
$5, free to members, or bring wine/snacks to share
Museum of the Living Artist
1439 El Prado, Balboa Park
Contact Michael Klam at 619-957-3264
or 619-236-0011, sandiego-art.org
learn more about the authors at
literature.ucsd.edu/people/faculty/rarmantrout.html
and edwindecker.com

Poetry Slam as Crushing Blow

gave the most money
to a guy who pandered all
the way to the top

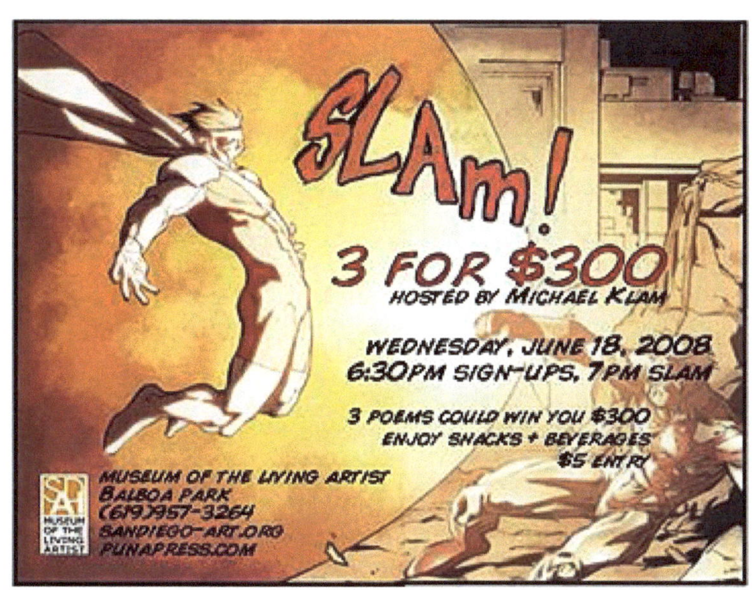
SLAm!
3 FOR $300
HOSTED BY MICHAEL KLAM
WEDNESDAY, JUNE 18, 2008
6:30PM SIGN-UPS, 7PM SLAM
3 POEMS COULD WIN YOU $300
ENJOY SNACKS + BEVERAGES
$5 ENTRY
MUSEUM OF THE LIVING ARTIST
BALBOA PARK
(619)957-3264
SANDIEGO-ART.ORG
PUNAPRESS.COM
MUSEUM OF THE LIVING ARTIST

Gill and Jerrica

my main music man
does not hug like Jerrica
but he sure can play

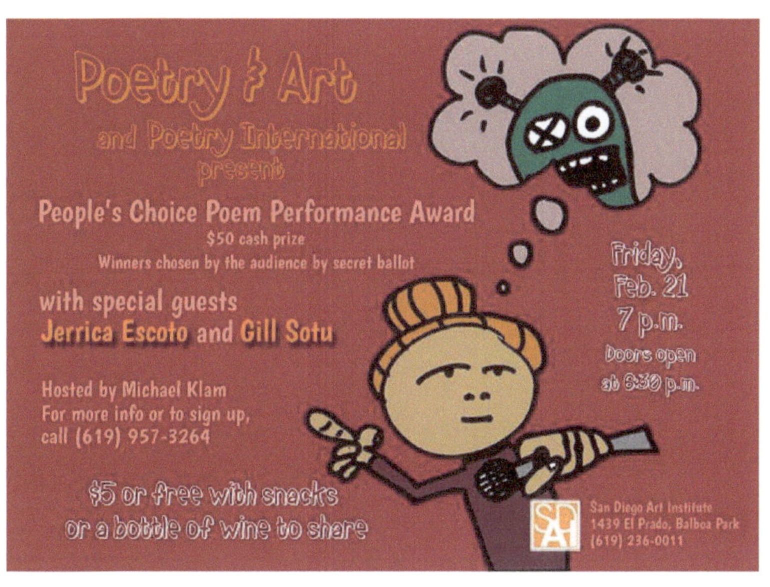
Poetry & Art
and Poetry International
present
People's Choice Poem Performance Award
$50 cash prize
Winners chosen by the audience by secret ballot
with special guests
Jerrica Escoto and Gill Sotu
Hosted by Michael Klam
For more info or to sign up,
call (619) 957-3264
$5 or free with snacks
or a bottle of wine to share
Friday,
Feb. 21
7 p.m.
Doors open
at 6:30 p.m.
SDAI
San Diego Art Institute
1439 El Prado, Balboa Park
(619) 236-0011

Bottled Narcissism

Mr U who as
an anthologist saw U's
far as eye could see

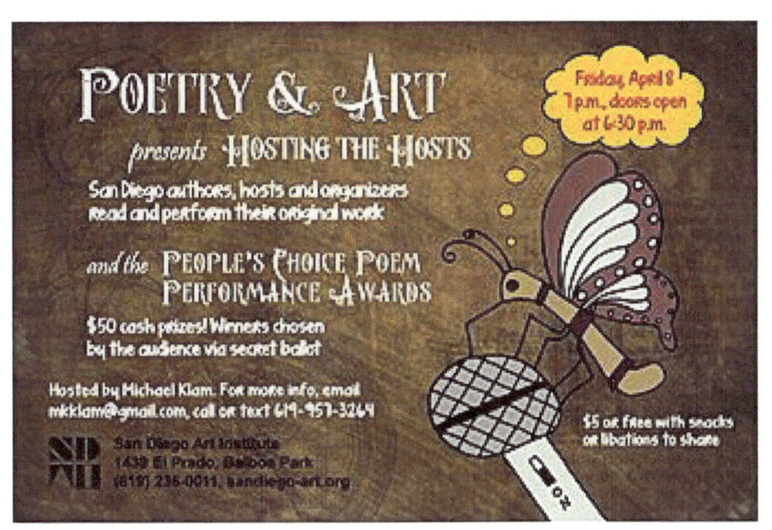

POETRY & ART
presents HOSTING THE HOSTS
San Diego authors, hosts and organizers
read and perform their original work
and the PEOPLE'S CHOICE POEM
PERFORMANCE AWARDS
$50 cash prizes! Winners chosen
by the audience via secret ballot
Hosted by Michael Klam. For more info, email
mkklam@gmail.com, call or text 619-957-3264
San Diego Art Institute
1439 El Prado, Balboa Park
(619) 236-0011, sandiego-art.org
Friday, April 8
7 p.m., doors open
at 6:30 p.m.
$5 or free with snacks
or libations to share

Best Poster Ever

Art Institute said,
"Want to play? You gotta pay!"
Narwhal shits money.

Poetry & Art
presents
Edwin Decker, Al Howard
Anna Zappoli Jenkins & Viet Mai
and the People's Choice Poem Performance Awards
Friday, Feb. 23
7 pm
Doors open at 6:30
Music by Gill Sotu | Hosted by Michael Klam
For more info or to sign up
visit poetryandartsd.com
email mkklam@gmail.com
call or text (619) 957-3264
$6 or free with snacks
or a bottle of wine to share
San Diego Art Institute
1439 El Prado, Balboa Park
(619) 236-0011

I Miss Charlene

Baldridge wrote like
her life depended on it
winter rose must sing

POETRY & ART

PRESENTS

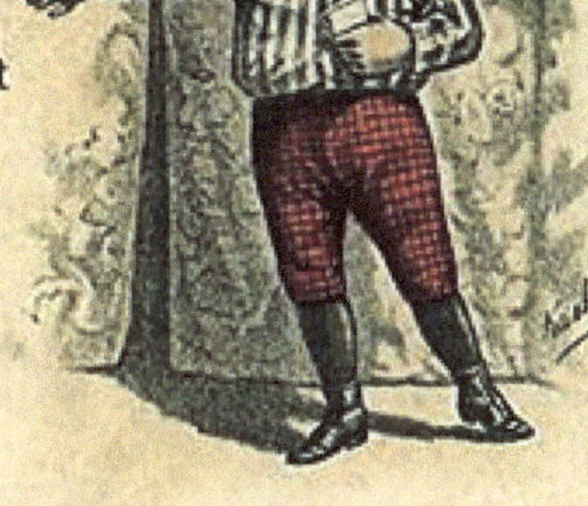

CHARLENE BALDRIDGE

San Diego theater critic and poet extraordinaire!

ZURI WATERS

installation artiste with verbal dicer and slicer J. Godley live!

NATHAN HUBBARD

percussionist and composer, like nothing you've ever heard! plus the mellifluous Shannon Perkins!

WEDNESDAY, JUNE 20, 2007

JUST FIVE DOLLARS!

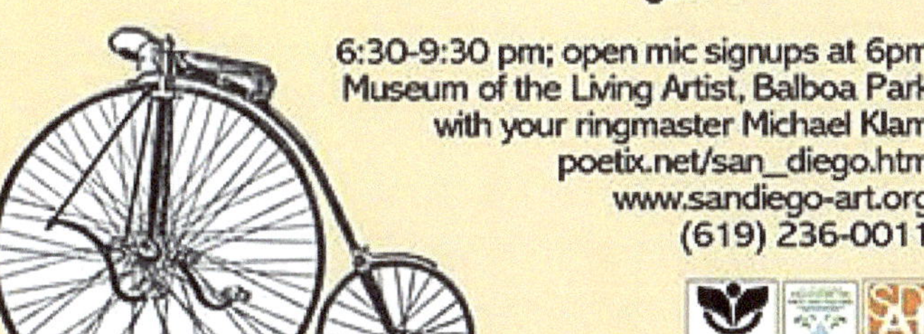

6:30-9:30 pm; open mic signups at 6pm
Museum of the Living Artist, Balboa Park
with your ringmaster Michael Klam
poetix.net/san_diego.htm
www.sandiego-art.org
(619) 236-0011

NATIONAL ENDOWMENT FOR THE ARTS

MUSEUM OF THE LIVING ARTIST

steve got all dressed up for the show

I point to Kowit's
sandwich stains on his sweatshirt
we laugh like two fools

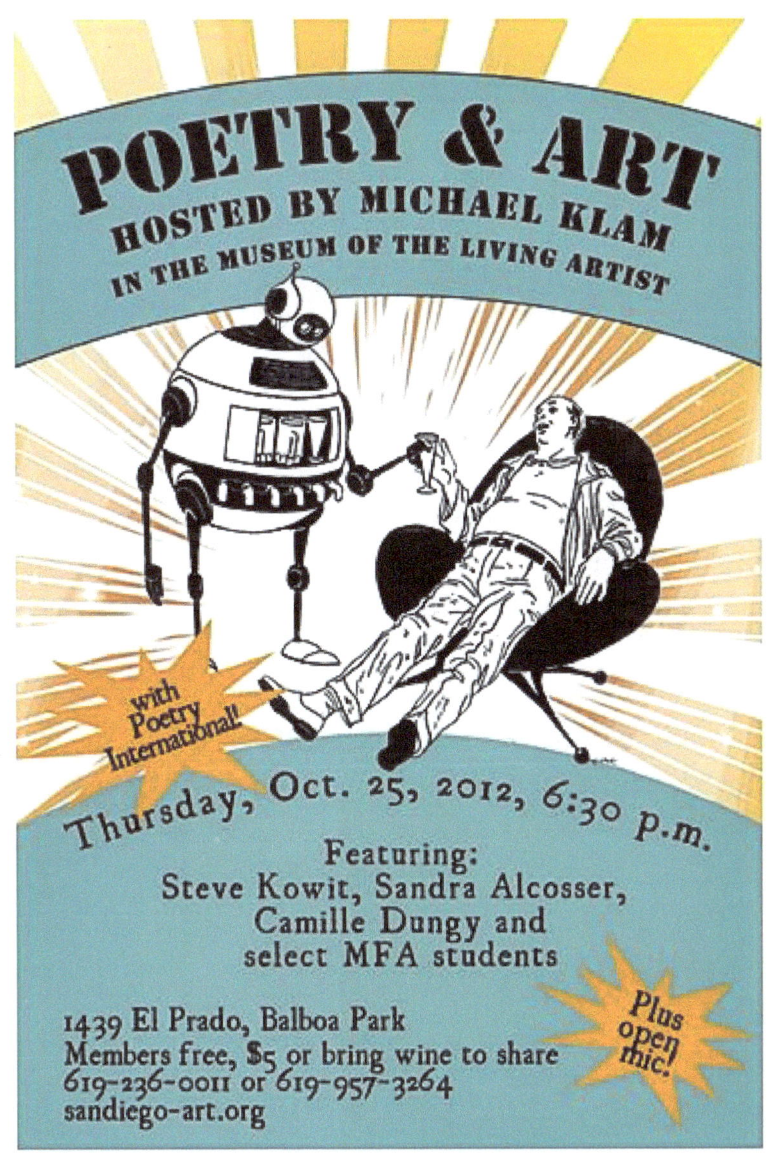
POETRY & ART
HOSTED BY MICHAEL KLAM
IN THE MUSEUM OF THE LIVING ARTIST
with Poetry International!
Thursday, Oct. 25, 2012, 6:30 p.m.
Featuring:
Steve Kowit, Sandra Alcosser,
Camille Dungy and
select MFA students
1439 El Prado, Balboa Park
Members free, $5 or bring wine to share
619-236-0011 or 619-957-3264
sandiego-art.org
Plus open mic!

WWJD?
Well, Probably Sit and Behold

This night we witnessed
fine art pole dance on a rood
XDrop biblical

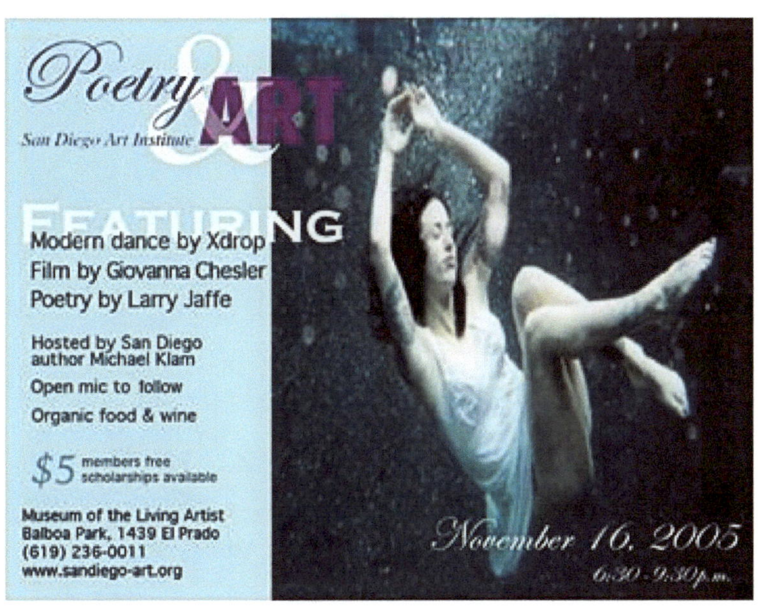
Poetry & ART
San Diego Art Institute
FEATURING
Modern dance by Xdrop
Film by Giovanna Chesler
Poetry by Larry Jaffe
Hosted by San Diego
author Michael Klam
Open mic to follow
Organic food & wine
$5 members free
scholarships available
Museum of the Living Artist
Balboa Park, 1439 El Prado
(619) 236-0011
www.sandiego-art.org
November 16, 2005
6:30 - 9:30p.m.

Go SD Poetry!

MFA poets
with so much talent and drive
hope for the future

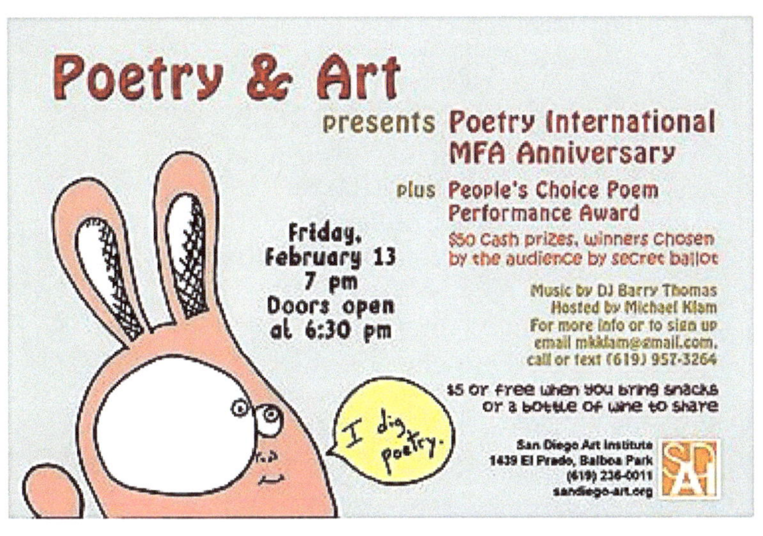
Poetry & Art
presents Poetry International
MFA Anniversary
plus People's Choice Poem
Performance Award
$50 Cash prizes, winners chosen
by the audience by secret ballot
Friday,
February 13
7 pm
Doors open
at 6:30 pm
Music by DJ Barry Thomas
Hosted by Michael Klam
For more info or to sign up
email mkklam@gmail.com,
call or text (619) 957-3264
$5 or free when you bring snacks
or a bottle of wine to share
I dig poetry.
San Diego Art Institute
1439 El Prado, Balboa Park
(619) 236-0011
sandiego-art.org

Radical Pedagogy

Graffiti Lucha
Artist, professor, poet
Shine controlled splatter

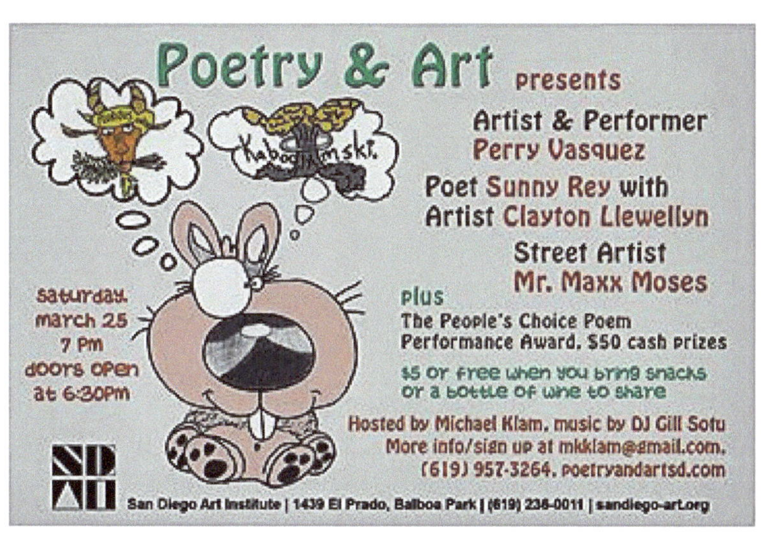
Poetry & Art presents
Artist & Performer
Perry Vasquez
Poet Sunny Rey with
Artist Clayton Llewellyn
Street Artist
Mr. Maxx Moses
saturday
march 25
7 pm
doors open
at 6:30pm
plus
The People's Choice Poem
Performance Award. $50 cash prizes
$5 or free when you bring snacks
or a bottle of wine to share
Hosted by Michael Klam. music by DJ Gill Sotu
More info/sign up at mkklam@gmail.com.
(619) 957-3264. poetryandartsd.com
San Diego Art Institute | 1439 El Prado, Balboa Park | (619) 236-0011 | sandiego-art.org

MOPA with Ted Washington
Packing Serious Heat

guns and ammo shop
is having a back-to-school
celebration sale

Karaoke Process Poem
for
Judy Reeves
and
Steve Montgomery

Judy/Steve Brain Child
Poetry Karaoke
Seven syllables

More
Selected P&A Poster/Flier Art

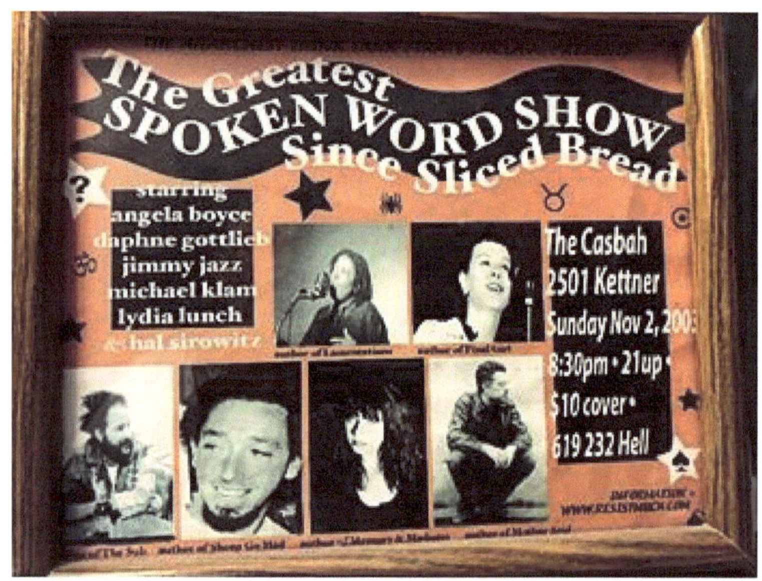

One from Jimmy Jazz with Love

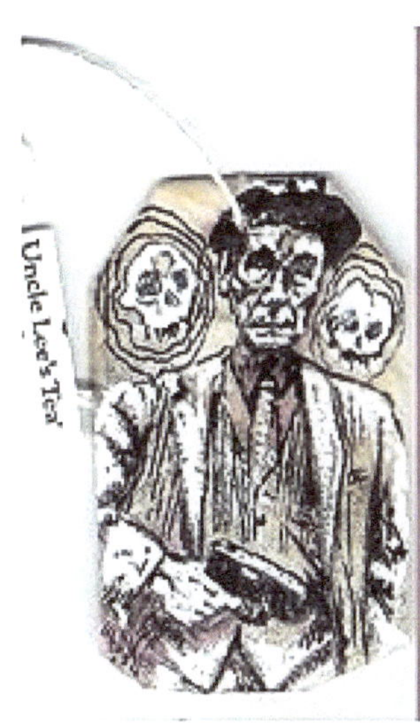

Poetry & Art Series 2017
Friday, Sept. 22

7pm, doors open at 6:30pm

Featuring

Tomas Gayton, Jim Moreno and Chris Vannoy

Plus

The People's Choice Poem Performance Awards
$50 cash prizes
Sign up at mkklam@gmail.com or 619-957-3264
poetryandartsd.com

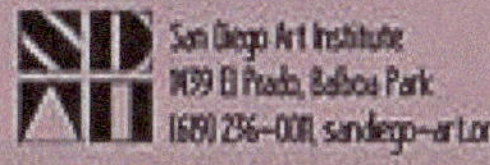

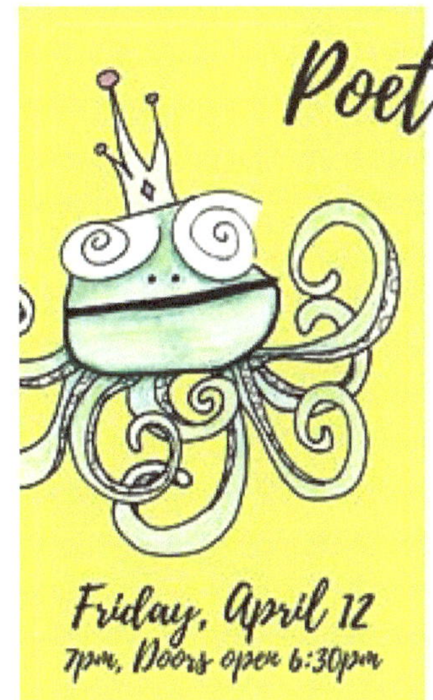

Poetry & Art

presents

CULTURES CONNECT

featuring

KIMBERLY DARK, MALACHI BLACK, MARIO DEMATTEO,
JENNIFER MINNITI-SHIPPEY, SHADAB ZEEST HASHMI,
MINERVA AND GERARDO NAVARRO, A.K.A. NEMONICO

plus

THREE $50 PEOPLE'S CHOICE PRIZES CHOSEN
BY THE AUDIENCE BY SECRET BALLOT

HOSTED BY MICHAEL KLAM AND JIM MORENO, MUSIC BY DJ GILL SOTU
POETRYANDARTSD.COM, MKKLAM@GMAIL.COM, (619) 957-3264

$6, MEMBERS FREE

San Diego Art Institute
1439 El Prado, Balboa Park
(619) 236-0011

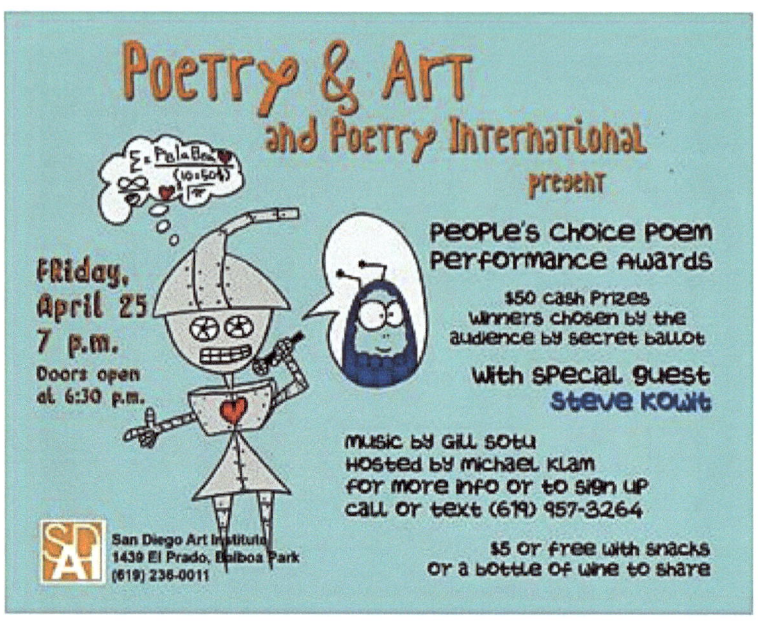

Poetry & Art
presents
Fiction International
Friday, March 1, 2013

Doors open
at 6:30pm

Featuring Harold Jaffe and Katie Farris
plus Jimmy Jazz

and readings by select FI assistant editors Julie Harris,
Ryan Forsythe, Dani Heinemeyer and Charlie Griggs

live music by Nathan Hubbard

Hosted by Michael Klam

5 dollars or bring a bottle of wine to share
and get in free

Museum of the Living Artist, 1439 El Prado, Balboa Park, 619-957-3264, sandiego-art.org

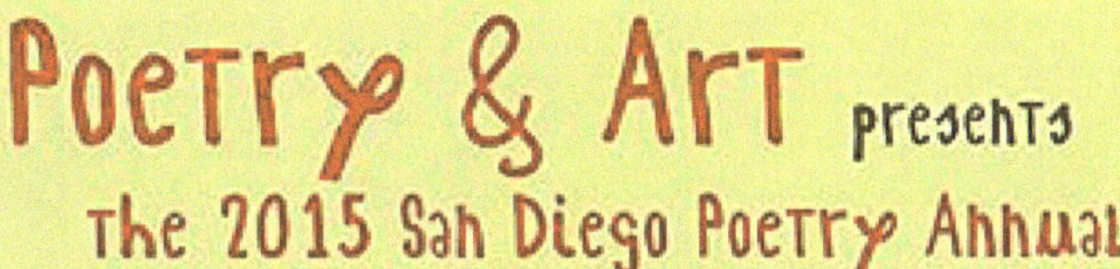

featuring

New Jersey poet Maria Mazziotti Gillan
and contributing authors from SDPA

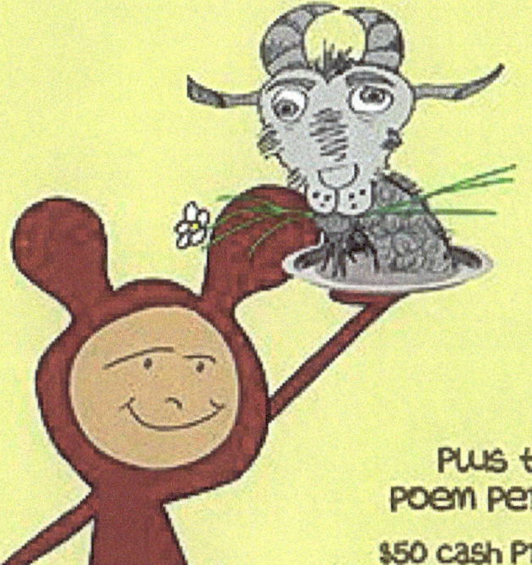

Saturday,
June 20
7 pm
Doors open
at 6:30 pm

Live Painting by
Perry Vasquez

Plus the People's Choice
Poem Performance Awards

$50 cash prizes. winners chosen
by the audience in a secret ballot

$5 or free with snacks
or libations to share

music by DJ Barry Thomas
hosted by Michael Klam
for more info or to sign up
call or text 619-957-3264

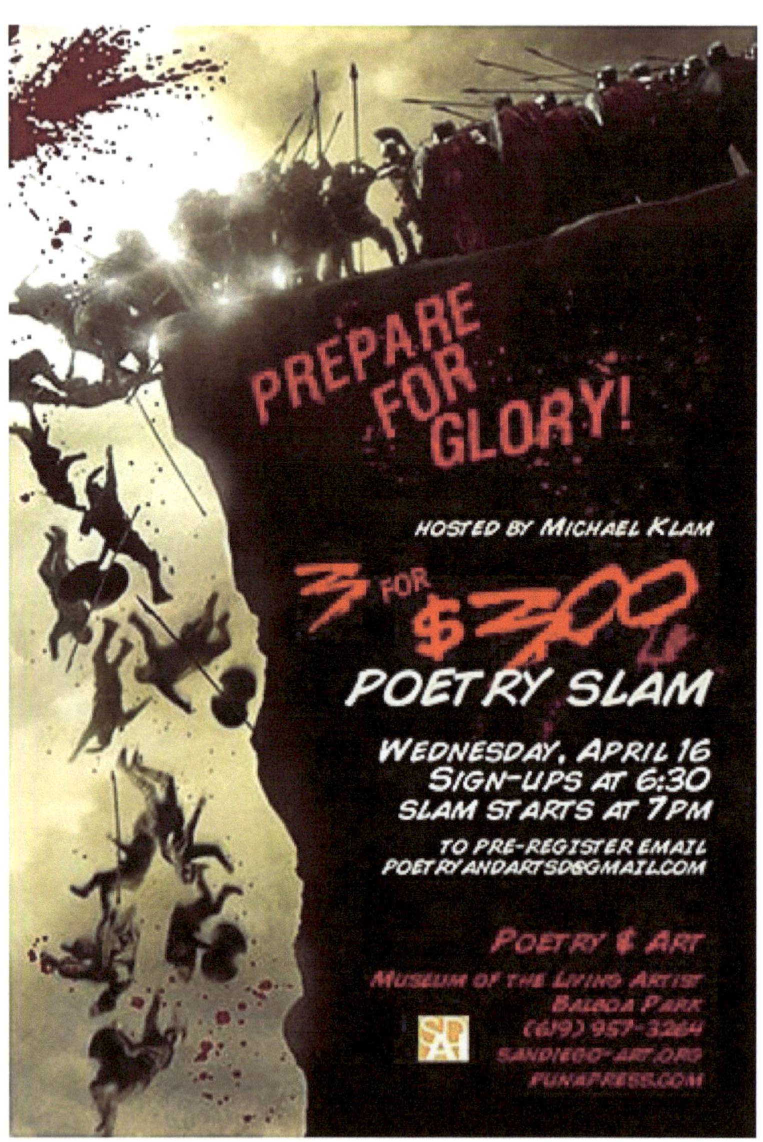
PREPARE FOR GLORY!
HOSTED BY MICHAEL KLAM
3 FOR $300
POETRY SLAM
WEDNESDAY, APRIL 16
SIGN-UPS AT 6:30
SLAM STARTS AT 7PM
TO PRE-REGISTER EMAIL
POETRYANDARTSD@GMAIL.COM
POETRY & ART
MUSEUM OF THE LIVING ARTIST
BALBOA PARK

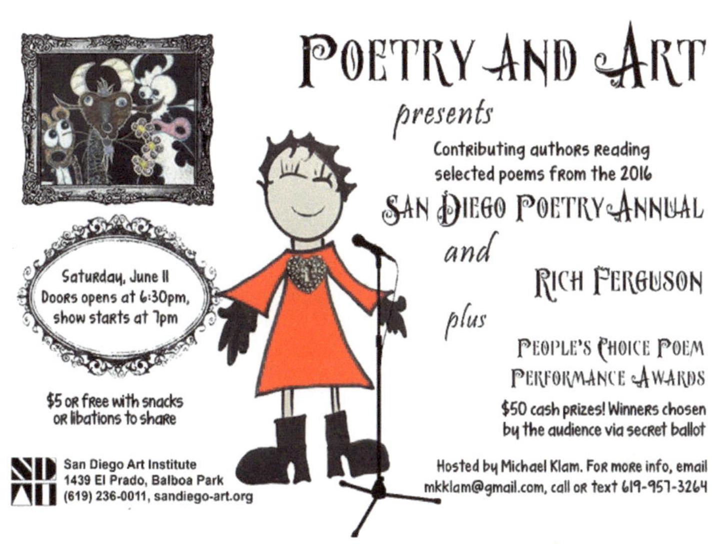
POETRY AND ART
presents
Contributing authors reading
selected poems from the 2016
SAN DIEGO POETRY ANNUAL
and
RICH FERGUSON
plus
PEOPLE'S CHOICE POEM
PERFORMANCE AWARDS
$50 cash prizes! Winners chosen
by the audience via secret ballot
Saturday, June 11
Doors opens at 6:30pm,
show starts at 7pm
$5 or free with snacks
or libations to share
San Diego Art Institute
1439 El Prado, Balboa Park
(619) 236-0011, sandiego-art.org
Hosted by Michael Klam. For more info, email
mkklam@gmail.com, call or text 619-957-3264

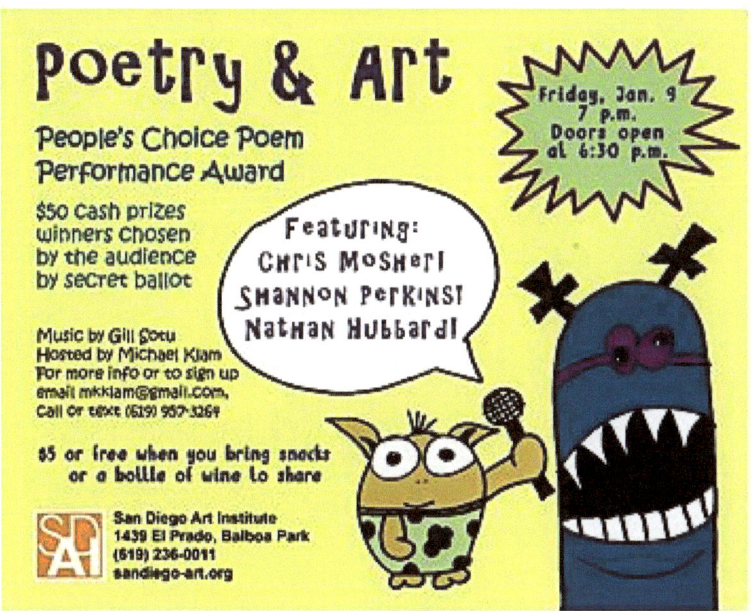
Poetry & Art
People's Choice Poem
Performance Award
$50 cash prizes
winners chosen
by the audience
by secret ballot
Friday, Jan. 9
7 p.m.
Doors open
at 6:30 p.m.
Featuring:
Chris Mosher!
Shannon Perkins!
Nathan Hubbard!
Music by Gill Sotu
Hosted by Michael Klam
For more info or to sign up
email mkklam@gmail.com,
Call or text (619) 957-3264
$5 or free when you bring snacks
or a bottle of wine to share
San Diego Art Institute
1439 El Prado, Balboa Park
(619) 236-0011
sandiego-art.org

Poetry & Art Series 2013 presents

an evening in translation with
Nikola Madzirov

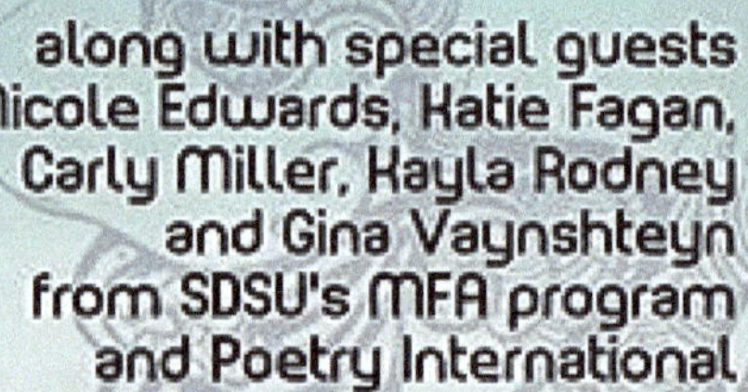

along with special guests
Nicole Edwards, Katie Fagan,
Carly Miller, Kayla Rodney
and Gina Vaynshteyn
from SDSU's MFA program
and Poetry International

open mic
music by DJ Gill Sotu
wine & snacks
hosted by Michael Klam

Thursday, Sept. 26 at 6:30 pm
$5, free to members or
bring a bottle of wine to get in free

Museum of the Living Artist, 1439 El Prado, Balboa Park
619-957-3264, sandiego-art.org

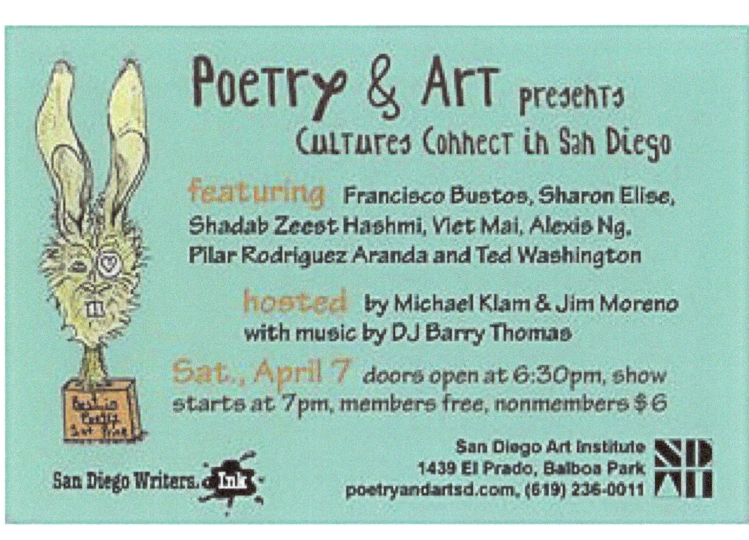
Poetry & Art presents
Cultures Connect in San Diego
featuring Francisco Bustos, Sharon Elise, Shadab Zeest Hashmi, Viet Mai, Alexis Ng, Pilar Rodriguez Aranda and Ted Washington
hosted by Michael Klam & Jim Moreno
with music by DJ Barry Thomas
Sat., April 7 doors open at 6:30pm, show starts at 7pm, members free, nonmembers $6
San Diego Art Institute
1439 El Prado, Balboa Park
poetryandartsd.com, (619) 236-0011
San Diego Writers, Ink

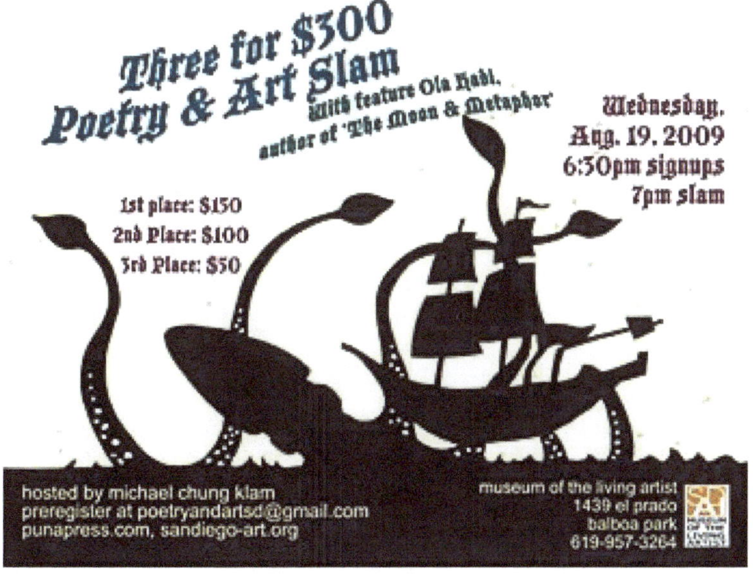
Three for $300
Poetry & Art Slam
with feature Ola Nabi,
author of 'The Moon & Metaphor'
Wednesday,
Aug. 19. 2009
6:30pm signups
7pm slam
1st place: $150
2nd Place: $100
3rd Place: $50
hosted by michael chung klam
preregister at poetryandartsd@gmail.com
punapress.com, sandiego-art.org
museum of the living artist
1439 el prado
balboa park
619-957-3264

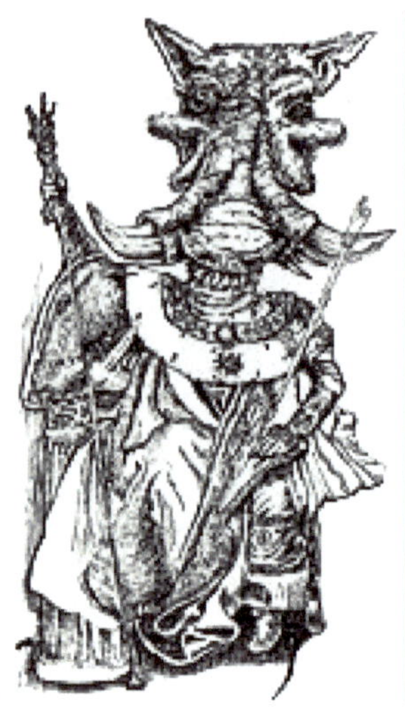

Poetry & Art Series 2017
Friday, Nov. 10

7pm, doors open at 6:30pm

Featuring

Tomas Gayton, Jim Moreno, Chris Vannoy
Sharon Elise and Ying Wu

Plus

The People's Choice Poem Performance Awards
$50 cash prizes
Music provided by DJ Barry Thomas
Sign up at mkklam@gmail.com or 619-957-3264
poetryandartsd.com

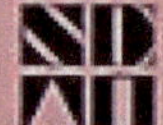

San Diego Art Institute
1439 El Prado, Balboa Park
(619) 236-0011, sandiego-art.org

Poetry & Art presents

the San Diego Poetry Annual featuring

Ameerah Holliday, Jill G. Hall, Robt O'Sullivan Schleith,
Chris Wakefield, Olga García, Billiekai Boughton
and contributors to SDPA 2017–18

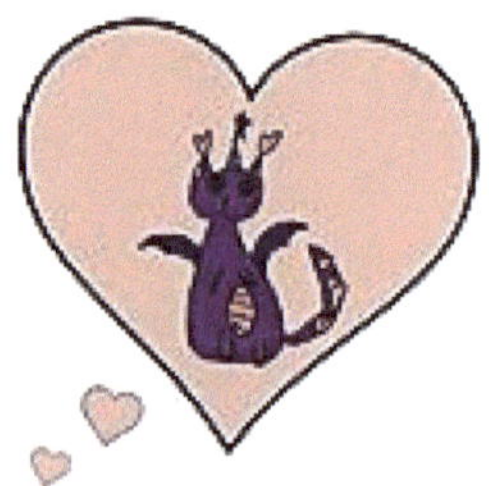

Hosted by Michael Klam
Music by Gill Sotu
For more info visit
poetryandartsd.com
email mkklam@gmail.com
call or text (619) 957-3264

Friday, June 29 @ 7 pm
Doors open at 6:30 pm
$6 or free for members

San Diego Art Institute
1439 El Prado, Balboa Park
(619) 236-0011

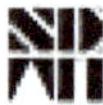

Afterword

Come pandemics and wildfires and closures and uncertainty...the Poetry & Art Series will remain steady and carry on. P&A will continue to grow and connect San Diego's extraordinary poetry community.

For now, poets and artists, we will see you online. To find upcoming events and info, please visit poetryandartsd.com, sandiegopoetryannual.com, and search for Broken Anchor Poetry.

About the Poet-Artist

Michael Klam is the Executive Editor of the *San Diego Poetry Annual* and a partner with the Border Voices Poetry Project and Broken Anchor Poetry.

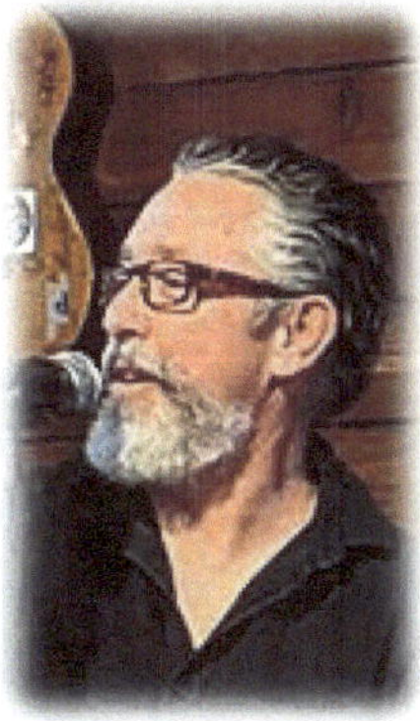

He edited the adult poetry section of the 2020 Border Voices anthology, *Springtime in Paradise*, and co-edited the San Diego Writers, Ink anthology, *A Year in Ink* [Volume 6].

Since 2001, he has organized and hosted the Poetry & Art Series, featuring acclaimed musicians, visual artists, dancers, and poets.

His books are *Emma and the Buddha Frog (2007)*, a San Diego Book Awards finalist, and *The Cheapest Flight to Paradise* (2018), both from Puna Press.

Acknowledgments

With thanks to so many across so much of our poetry community:

San Diego Poetry Annual

Bill Harding, Anthony Blacksher,
Seretta Martin, Ameerah Holliday

Puna Press

Ted Washington

Broken Anchor Poetry

Ying Wu, Andy Palasciano

Poetry & Art Series

Jennifer Klam, Jimmy Jazz, Gill Sotu,
Poetry International/SDSU MFA interns and volunteers

Poetry Karaoke

Judy Reeves, Steven Montgomery, Marc Chery

Central Library Local Author's Showcase

Linda Brawley, Marc Chery

Mentors/Partners

Sharon Elise, Bill Harding,
Jack Webb/*Border Voices*, Ted Washington

Credits

Cover art: MICHAEL KLAM

Interior art and fliers: MICHAEL, JENNIFER, and ANYA KLAM

Teabag Burroughs (p. 95) and *King Beast* (p. 102) images: RON MOYA

www.ingramcontent.com/pod-product-compliance
Lightning Source LLC
LaVergne TN
LVHW052305100826
845147LV00006B/683